OWNING THE FUTURE

OWNING THE FUTURE

Power and Property in an Age of Crisis

Adrienne Buller and Mathew Lawrence

VERSO

London • New York

First published by Verso 2022
© Adrienne Buller and Mathew Lawrence 2022

1 3 5 7 9 10 8 6 4 2

Verso
UK: 6 Meard Street, London W1F 0EG
US: 388 Atlantic Avenue, Brooklyn, NY 11217
versobooks.com

Verso is the imprint of New Left Books

ISBN-13: 978-1-83976-580-3
ISBN-13: 978-1-83976-583-4 (US EBK)
ISBN-13: 978-1-83976-582-7 (UK EBK)

British Library Cataloguing in Publication Data
A catalogue record for this book is available from the British Library

Library of Congress Cataloging-in-Publication Data
A catalog record for this book is available from the Library of Congress

Typeset in Garamond by Biblichor Ltd, Edinburgh
Printed and bound by CPI Group (UK) Ltd, Croydon, CR0 4YY

Contents

Introduction

Power, Property, and a Pandemic

The concept of progress must be grounded in the idea of catastrophe. That things are 'status quo' is the catastrophe.
— Walter Benjamin

In January 2021, the US secretary of the treasury Janet Yellen declared that the United States was facing 'four historic crises', of which Covid-19 was just one. 'In addition to the pandemic, the US is also facing a climate crisis, a crisis of systemic racism, and an economic crisis that has been building for fifty years.' Yellen is far from a radical, but her diagnosis was correct. We live in an era of systemic and interconnected crises, which demands that our thinking be as 'radical as reality itself'.

Throughout the pandemic, the news cycle has been gripped by a series of mounting disasters. Global vaccine apartheid, the result of the Global North's refusal to allow non-proprietary sharing of vaccine technology, meant that by late 2021 80 percent of adults in the EU were fully vaccinated, but only 9.5 percent of people in low-income countries had received a single dose.[1] As housing wealth surged to record highs, renters endured ongoing insecurity.

As up to 500 million people were thrown into extreme poverty, with the incomes of 99 percent of the world's population falling between March 2020 and October 2021, the wealth of the world's 10 richest men doubled to $1.5 trillion, and a new billionaire was minted every 17 hours. Amid these plummeting incomes, the pandemic has supercharged the age of BlackRock: in late 2021 the world's leading asset manager topped $10 trillion in assets under management, a jump of more than $1 trillion from the year prior. And throughout this period of acute crisis, the climate and ecological emergencies have continued to unfurl at astonishing pace: 'once-in-a-lifetime' fires raged across Greece and the Pacific Northwest, while temperatures in Jacobabad, Pakistan surpassed the livable threshold for humans for the first time, a full decade ahead of scientific projections.

None of these are isolated. Rather, they are the fruits of a particular social and economic arrangement, one that has ripened over centuries. The crises we face today are both overlapping and unevenly felt, and running through each of them is an essential thread: the organising force of ownership. The pandemic set alight the mass of dry tinder piled up over decades in which the rights of property have been prioritised over collective well-being.

Power is intimately patterned by the distribution and nature of property rights. Thus, how our economy is owned, and in whose interest this power is exercised, decisively shapes our societies and our lives. This may seem like an obvious point; after all, property relations and the distribution of property have always been a vital determinant of how an economy is structured and whose interests it serves. We are hardly the first to suggest this, nor will we be the last. However, it is an insight that offers some hope. Ownership is not the sole determinant of social and economic outcomes, but it is a thread that connects the immense challenges we face, as well as the many ways in which we might strive to overcome them: by reimagining and transforming ownership.

Not-So-Unprecedented Times

The importance and organising power of ownership can be seen clearly in the pledges from the world's high-income economies to pursue some form of 'green recovery' from the pandemic, alongside cobbled-together plans to 'Build Back Better'. While many hint towards a recognition of the structural weaknesses in our societies and economies, these plans, to date, offer no path to resolving the underlying structures that made them so vulnerable to the impacts of the crisis in the first place. They declare unprecedented times only to pursue the same path as before.

This durable commitment to status quo policy is not unrelated to the fact that, as we write this in the summer of 2021, the state of the global financial markets gives no indication of the turmoil of the past eighteen months. Buoyed by central bank and fiscal interventions, many stock market indexes closed 2020 at record highs, utterly divorced from the upheaval that most were experiencing. Then, as US president Joe Biden presented his infrastructure package and announced his intention for the US to become a world leader in electric vehicles, and Boris Johnson touted the prospect of battery 'gigafactories' dotting the UK, the financial press began speculating that the world had entered a new 'commodity supercycle', which would see booming demand for years to come in everything from metals to forestry. Investors looked at the array of 'Build Back Betters' pouring out of Europe, the UK, and the US, and saw dollar signs.

At the heart of these fiscal stimulus plans, however 'green', lurks a commitment to superficially 'greening' our economies as they are, rather than reckoning with the governing logics, institutions, and profound inequalities in wealth and power that create the conditions for ecological devastation.[2] The result? Between a promised boom in electric vehicles (EVs) and an anticipated rise in energy use, the International Energy Agency predicts global demand for lithium (required for batteries and grid storage) will increase more than forty-fold by 2040. Unfortunately, when we look under the hood of the coming battery boom, promises of 'green recovery' quickly sour. Amid record droughts across the Atacama salt flats, currently a primary source of lithium for the global economy, sparse water supplies are increasingly diverted from local communities to meet the demands of the extractive industry. Long before the pandemic hit, the immense legal privileges endowed on multinational corporations – enshrined in trade agreements and enforced by courts favouring the prerogatives of private enterprise – had allowed them to turn Indigenous communities and many territories in the Global South into sacrifice zones for capitalist centres and interests. As these same centres look to revive faltering economies with 'green recoveries', these two-tiered borders will only harden.[3]

The threat of expropriation underlying plans for 'green recoveries', however, is just one avenue through which the contradictions of existing property relations have generated crisis and injustice, and will continue to do so as further crises unfold. Unequal access to vaccines underscores the tension between the needs of public health and the priorities of Big Pharma, which imposes false scarcity through the power of property. The inequalities of the housing market, and insecurity it generates, painfully highlight the unfairness of making access to a secure home increasingly conditional on owning housing wealth rather than guaranteed as a social right. The rise of behemoth asset management firms with universal and concentrated shareholding challenges fundamental assumptions about how the corporation, the engine of the global economy, is and should be governed. And arguably the most fundamental tension of all is the extreme concentration of wealth and control that enables a fraction of the population to consume and discard a majority of the world's resources and enclose the atmospheric commons: its shared and finite ability to withstand the weight of rising carbon.

In many senses, the contemporary capitalist system is ruthlessly effective, doing precisely what it is designed to do: accumulate, enclose, concentrate and expand for the benefit of those who own. It has generated extraordinary wealth, but in doing so has made its hallmark poverty amid unprecedented plenty. Now, the same processes of concentration, enclosure, and extraction built into its design are beginning to exhaust the very sources of social and ecological wealth that capitalist economies rely upon to reproduce themselves. The tremendous explosion of wealth over the course of the twentieth century brought with it profoundly damaged ecosystems, from the Colorado River's near exhaustion to the death of the Catete River in Brazil under the weight of heavy metal runoff, while its production has continued to impoverish, oppress, and exploit communities from the

Standing Rock Sioux to the garment workers of Leicester
and Bangladesh. Environmental plunder, vaccine nationalism, enormously concentrated economic power – these are best
understood as products of the same foundation: the claims
of exclusive and hierarchical ownership against the world.
Ours is an economic model rooted in a particular ownership
regime dominated by private control. By dispossessing individuals from access to the resources they need to live outside
of the market, the world's majority must sell their labour
power for a wage to another, much smaller, class – the
owners of capital – to survive. This arrangement inscribes
class divisions and domination into social relations, between
the owners of capital and their managerial allies and the
comparatively propertyless majority, whether waged or
unwaged. It's this constitutive role in shaping how an
economy operates and in whose interest that has meant
patterns of property and ownership have strongly shaped
the unfolding of the pandemic, making this 'great equaliser'
so profoundly unequal.

Covid-19 may have been a crisis without precedent in our
lifetimes so far, but it will not be the last. We are now living
through the most stable conditions many of us are likely to
experience in our lives. Ecological crisis is accelerating and
compounding. More than two-thirds of the world's wildlife
has been lost since 1970.[4] Farmed poultry now makes up
70 percent of all bird life on Earth.[5] Permafrost in the arctic
is thawing 70 years ahead of predictions, releasing potentially catastrophic quantities of climate-warming methane
into the air.[6] The Sixth Assessment Report of the Inter-
governmental Panel on Climate Change concluded that the
world is on track to soar past 1.5 degrees Celsius of warming
as early as 2030 – a threshold which, if unreversed, will

subject millions more to increased drought, famine, sea-level rise, and untold disasters every year by 2100. For many, overwhelmingly in the Global South, this crisis is already underway. The enclosure of our personal data and mono-polisation of technological infrastructures generates new billionaires with startling regularity even as the digital divide grows. Despite an explosion of pharmaceutical patents, tuberculosis (a curable disease that overwhelmingly impacts the global poor) remains the world's deadliest infectious disease. Meanwhile the comparative unprofitability of developing new antibiotics means life-saving medicine goes undeveloped, even as rates of resistance surge, which could make routine surgeries and chemotherapy untenable.[7]

Within this context, rhetorical commitment to building a more equal, just, and ecologically sustainable economy without durably transforming property relations rings hollow. This is not to say certain progressive reforms and efforts to break out from economic stagnation are not, in the context of immediate suffering, welcome steps in the right direction. But it is to insist on their limits. Unless accompanied by a thoroughgoing transformation of ownership and control, the result of these efforts will at best secure moderate redistribution without prising open the more fundamental questions beneath: what should the priority of our economies be? How can we ensure democratic power determines the trajectory of economic development? How can we organise society around meeting needs instead of accumulation and the exclusionary expansion of unequal private wealth?

If the slogan of capital's revolt in the 1970s was 'Stabilise prices, crush labour, discipline the south',[8] the (admittedly bulkier) slogan of the politics aiming to end its rule should instead proclaim: 'Democratise the economy, decommodify the foundations of life, defend the commons.' Democratise! Decommodify! Defend! Underlying this refrain is an effort to bring to life Aaron Benanav's insight that 'abundance is not a technological threshold but a social relationship'.[9] In short, we have the resources and capabilities, today, to guarantee material security and the fundamentals of a good life for everyone on Earth. There is no need to wait for some imagined technological liberation, nor justification for doing so. Democratising ownership can redistribute power and the gains of collective enterprise; decommodifying provision of the goods and infrastructures we need can free us from market dependency while ensuring everyone has access to life's necessities; and by defending and expanding the commons, we can steward shared assets for the common good. What follows is an account of why and how to break decisively with an increasingly unstable economic system based on the conceit that the rich complexity of human societies and natural systems is best governed through private property claims, with social life coercively structured by market relations themselves enforced by state power.[10]

This is ultimately a project of democracy: of the extension of democratic principles and relationships into spaces currently ruled by the entitlements of private property. If neoliberalism is a project of state power to defend the prerogatives of property against popular demands for more equal reordering, the counter-movement insists instead that 'the economy' is a socially made entity that democratic power can restructure. This is not 'democratisation' in some abstract or superficial sense; rather, a democratic economy is one where the principles of democracy with which we are all familiar extend beyond the political system and into our workplaces and communities, and where we re-extend common control over how the economy functions in service of expanding human freedom. As Amnar Akbar argues, this must not just redistribute resources to meet needs that neither state nor market currently provide; it must democratise power, ensuring 'people possess the agency and power to self-determine the conditions of their lives . . . a say in how we spend our collective wealth, how we relate to the land, and how we reimagine the infrastructure in which we live'.[11] That agenda is the subject of this book. Admittedly, it must advance across unstable terrain. Faith in democratic systems is on the wane, particularly among the young.[12] The intense pressures of the pandemic both condensed and amplified pre-existing trends, while opening up new contradictions. At the collapsing boundary between the economic and political, public power has once again backstopped private wealth.

The first challenge is to imagine this agenda – and the second to identify the sites of agency and the strategies that can realise it. We believe a future of genuine security for all, one that has broken decisively with the primacy of private property over planetary stability and human and non-human well-being, is wholly attainable (if not easily won). It may be true that 'it's easier to imagine the end of the world than the end of capitalism' – and indeed, this may be the choice we are facing. It's not, however, impossible, particularly if we recognise that the world we want is founded on interests and values that the majority share: democracy, justice, equality, freedom.

The seeds of this different world are already there. To that end, we hope what follows can contribute to the cohering of such a vision. It is neither a manifesto nor an exhaustive exposition of all that is wrong with our economies and societies, and what collective effort could make right. We do hope, however, that by exploring the role of particular forms of ownership in fettering our potential, it can be a resource to help marry the principles of a radically different vision for the world with the agency of immediate tools and points of leverage to set us on that path.[13]

I

Ownership Matters

The naturalization of capitalism . . . limits our understanding of the past. At the same time, it restricts our hopes and expectations for the future, for if capitalism is the natural culmination of history then surmounting it is unimaginable. But capitalism is not natural. People have made it. And what we have made, we can change.
— Ellen Meiksins Wood, *The Origin of Capitalism*

How a society operates, and in whose interests, is fundamentally shaped by who owns and controls its productive wealth. Baronial possession of land shaped feudalism, colonial dispossesion underpinned the accumulation of empire, the ownership of human beings by other human beings created the phenomenal wealth and appalling violence of slaver societies, and still today it is the interests of asset owners that largely dictate how our economies are run and our resources organised. These structures evolved over time; neither neutral nor fixed, the rules governing property rights reflect the ebb and flow of power and class relations within a society. But what exactly constitutes ownership, and why does it matter?

Ownership is a complex and in many ways overlapping

and contingent concept. It implies the possession of a set of enforceable rights over defined property, assets, and resources in which the owner holds the ultimate interest. In Anglo-American capitalism,[1] ownership of property and income-generating assets typically confers, at least in the popular sense of the term, the 'right to use resources exclusively without much acknowledgement of (especially the more systemic) externalities produced by such behaviour'.[2] Regardless of the consequences that follow from ownership of a specific thing or asset, whether exploitation or environmental destruction, ownership is taken to grant the owner the ability to use resources exclusively and extensively for their benefit. Property rules universalise the ability of an owner to exclude others from the control or benefit of assets and resources, while appropriating the rewards.

Ownership is therefore inherently relational. It empowers the propertied at the expense of the propertyless, imposing duties on the latter to benefit the former. Importantly, this introduces a paradox of freedom: ownership's inherent exclusivity transforms what is a potentially common resource into a source of dispossession and insecurity for some, and economic empowerment, wealth, and comparative freedom for others.[3] The right of property, understood as control over the owned object or asset, generates a power of command and authority through ownership. In the process, it institutionalises an unequal and often unfree relation between people over resources. The way that we arrange and distribute property relations and ownership therefore shapes how power is held and production organised. Ownership 'underpins all other societal values and interactions, including our relationships to each other, as well as to work, to the rest of the world, and to nature'.[4]

There are many overlapping combinations of ownership, control, and governance that open or foreclose particular ways of organising our economies and societies. Our crisis-riddled world centres a particular form of private ownership: the large for-profit corporation, controlled by and for a nexus of executives, asset managers, and wealthy shareholders, within a shrinking oligopoly of companies, concentrating wealth and power in the hands of a few. This regime of ownership and the property rules undergirding it are created by the state through a combination of legislation and the implicit backstop of coercive enforcement. The way these rules are defined – setting out what can be owned, who can own, what can be done with property, how those rights and rules are enforced, and how property can move between different owners[5] – is both intensely political and systemically pivotal. Understanding the conjoined crises we face therefore requires us to confront our current ownership regime.

From Absolutes to Bundles

Ownership is often discussed – in the media, among policy-makers, or in our daily interactions – as entailing some kind of absolute or 'natural' right for exclusive use and control of an asset or resource; however, the reality is more complicated. Modern property rights emerged in pre-democratic societies and were intimately linked to histories of colonial violence and empire-building. As Timothy Mitchell has argued, the presentation of the primacy of property rights as the self-evidently correct institutional framework for organising economic and social life masks the violent and ongoing histories of constructing and maintaining property – 'of power, discipline, coercion, and dispossession' – that have prioritised ownership claims over other competing social demands and obligations.[6] Moreover, even if property claims were originally conceived as private, absolute, and wholly exclusive, they are now better thought of as a 'bundle of rights linking, through a complex set of social and legal relationships, the owner to other people . . . broken down and recomposed according to the situations and times concerned'.[7] In other words, they are the product not of some 'natural' and prior right, but a complex bundle of legal rules whose content is socially defined, and which varies by context.[8] Very often, those rights have been defined by the powerful in ways that reinforce and reproduce their position; crucially, however, this also makes them inherently contestable.

Ownership claims can take many forms: financial wealth, pension wealth, real estate wealth, physical wealth, for example – all of which can generate income from and entitlements of control over assets and resources. While you may have an absolute right over personal property, for instance over the book that you are holding in your hands, this absoluteness is rarely the case in questions of economic ownership. Property rights are often disaggregated, with control exercised by actors other than those who ultimately hold the economic interest. Take the pension system. The ultimate beneficiary – you or me, say, to whom money is ultimately due – may 'own' the underlying economic interest of the asset, such as a stock, in which our money is invested, but the other rights that derive from this ownership, such as governance rights within the corporation whose shares our money has helped purchase, are typically dispersed along a chain of financial intermediaries, such as pension fund trustees and asset managers.

In short, property rights are not unchangeable or pre-social. The processes that have created property rights were (and remain) contingent. Their creation has often been violent and ad hoc, and typically privileges the claims of the powerful over particular places or assets against competing interests. In other words, property rights are politically constituted and publicly maintained artefacts of convention, not 'natural rights'. As political philosopher Martin O'Neill argues,

> both the ownership societies of previous centuries and the hypercapitalist societies of the current era have depended on an aberrant, unjustifiable and ultimately destructive ideological mistake that treats property as something 'sacred', granting a kind of unwarranted normative authority to a mere social convention which ought to be malleable, and available to be moulded for the benefit of society at large.[9]

With all this in mind, it becomes easy to recognise the ideological gymnastics behind the perspective that prevails today whereby, for instance, taxation or other state intervention to challenge or redistribute market-derived wealth is seen as an indefensible intrusion on the natural prerogatives of private property. If property is first and foremost a social product, nurtured through a complex web of relationships and institutions, these claims make little sense. Existing distributions of wealth and income are only made possible by a system of property rights, entitlements, and markets that are themselves made possible by socially licensed government action to both create and enforce them. 'Private property' is thus both created and preserved by collective action.[10] Rather than interference in some pre-political

natural property right, then, taxation and similar interventions are just another part of the continual rearrangement
of economic claims that society and state undertake – a
rearrangement that should be judged on its efficacy and
equity in the current context, not held as permanent and
beyond the scope of revision.

Ownership is thus indivisible from politics and the collective ordering of our unequal world. It both reflects and
reinforces power and class relations at any given moment
and in any given place. The form and distribution of ownership coordinates and allocates economic claims between
labour and capital, between the commons and the propertied, and between the public and private spheres. The fact
that economic claims on societal wealth currently prioritise
asset holders is a reflection of 'bargaining power all the
way down'.[11] German public companies offer an interesting
example in this respect: their stock market valuations are
noticeably lower than similar companies in Anglo-American
capitalist economies. This is not because they are necessarily
less valuable or productive (very often it is quite the opposite);
it is because 'German households exercise more of their
claims on the business sector as workers rather than as wealth
owners'.[12] The emphasis on distribution of income through
social rights or wages, not ownership claims, reflects the
specific institutional arrangements and history of German
political economy, rather than immutable laws of property.
Similar examples, such as rent controls to constrict the
ownership rights of landlords, or public ownership to remove
private property claims through universalising non-market
access to health care, point to the diversity of forms that
ownership can take – and its unique ability to pattern
income, wealth, and power. Once we recognise that the

primacy of private property is not natural or inevitable, the issue then becomes, in the words of the political economists Andrew Gamble and Gavin Kelly, 'where the line should be drawn between the rights of private property and social control'.[13] These lines have been drawn by the law through political processes; they can just as readily be changed.

Freedom, Democracy, Justice?

Capitalist property relations confer power and profit on those who own and those who organise production on their behalf, while subjecting the propertyless to pervasive forms of domination and unfreedom. The result is a deeply illiberal and unequal regime premised, as Katharina Pistor argues, 'on private parties using the power of property the law confers on them to turn it into a means of extraction, and not only of labour, but also of social resources, including the financial safety nets that central banks provide, and even of law itself'.[14] To justify the extraordinary prerogatives and privileges that this ownership model confers – and the inequalities it generates – most point to the positive effects that it has on economic activity, and the claim that it advances principles of freedom, democracy, and justice.

There is some merit in this, and clearly transparency, security, and accountability are important factors in the design and reform of ownership regimes. However, current arrangements of ownership and governance undergird, in the words of Mike Davis, 'capitalism's inability to generate incomes for the majority of humanity, to provide jobs and meaningful social roles, end fossil fuel emissions, and translate revolutionary biological advances into public health. These are convergent crises, inseparable from one another.'[15]

Any full and honest account of the effects of prevailing property relations on the global economy will find our system fails resolutely to provide the security and dignity we all deserve – and which we have the capacity to provide. At the same time, principles at the heart of liberalism – of freedom, democracy, and justice – are systematically violated by capitalist property relations and the racialised, classed relations of exploitation they generate through their institutionalisation of three essential dynamics: concentration, exclusion, and constantly expanding enclosure.

As the political philosopher G. A. Cohen wrote, 'To think of capitalism as a realm of freedom is to overlook half of its nature.'[16] Property ownership, by definition, endows new freedoms on the owner, 'but it no less necessarily withdraws liberty from those who do not own'. It is a relation between parties that serves as a code for the enforcement of excludable claims between them. In this way, it writes exclusion into the rulebook of everyday life. Taking freedom seriously therefore means recognising that the nature and distribution of property rights is a way of assigning not just freedom but *unfreedom*. By privileging private economic property and contract even – and indeed routinely – at the expense of individual and collective well-being, we subject ordinary people to systematic unfreedom in their lives, in their workplaces, and in their communities.[17] Work therefore becomes a site of alienation and unfreedom for many, rooted in the division between the propertied and the working majority whose time is organised for the enrichment of others.

It is in this nexus that the strange union between conservatism (for which an inconsistent and highly unequal form of 'freedom' is a core mantra) and the unwavering defence of capitalism resides. Here, the priorities of economic elites and reactionary social forces are arranged in an uneasy alliance against the threat of rejection by the poor and the marginalised of the hierarchies that order and limit their freedom, with these energies redirected towards migrants or other marginalised groups.[18] If, as Frank Wilhoit astutely observed, conservatism's central proposition is that 'there must be in-groups whom the law protects but does not bind, alongside out-groups whom the law binds but does not protect', then property is structurally vital in generating this boundary.

A deep, universal freedom would imply a form far beyond our current freedoms to own and consume. It would be based on an expansion of an individual and communal liberty, not contingent on the oppression of others. It would require guaranteeing material security for all, without which dependency is assured. Delivering this freedom would mean coming to terms with and moving beyond the foundational unfreedoms that capitalist property relations generate. That will need new forms of economic coordination based on mutuality and democratic control, working towards justice in social and environmental relations over exchange value and unequal accumulation, and recognising, as Kathi Weeks has said, that 'freedom is a social – and hence necessarily political – endeavour'.[19]

Democracy, meanwhile, is rooted in the belief 'that people should be able to decide the conditions of their own lives to the fullest extent possible'.[20] Yet existing forms of ownership draw the boundary between social and private spheres in ways that exclude crucial decisions from democratic control, whether that is the constituency of the workplace, the community, or even humanity at large, inhibiting collective participation in decision-making over how resources and institutions should be arranged and used. As Hadas Thier argues, this points to the 'contradiction at the heart of democracy under capitalism; that the most fundamental realm of life – how we produce and reproduce the world around us through labour – is always kept out of democratic reach'.[21] Perhaps most fundamentally, private control of investment gives the owners of assets and their managerial allies enormous power. As Nancy Fraser writes: 'How a society uses its surplus capacities is absolutely central, raising fundamental questions about how people want to live – where they choose to invest their collective energies, how they propose to balance "productive work" vis-à-vis family life, leisure and other activities – as well as how they aspire to relate to non-human nature and what they aim to leave to future generations.'[22] The privatisation of this power – based on wealth, not participation, and directed towards capital accumulation for asset owners, not the meeting of social needs – is an extraordinary ceding of control over the future from the many to the few.

In a socially just society, everyone would have 'broadly equal access to the necessary material and social means to live flourishing lives'.[23] This is tragically far from our global reality, even within the world's highest-income economies. In the UK, for example, despite benefiting from being near the apex of an extractive and unequal global economy, a third of the population fell below the minimum income standard during the pandemic,[24] and a devastating 4 million children were living in poverty even before it began.[25] In a global economy marked by profound inequality, where according to Credit Suisse, the richest 1 percent own 43.4 percent of the world's wealth, we continue to fall woefully short of providing basic material security for all despite some (often exaggerated) advances,[26] cementing a society and economy defined by injustice. The aftershocks of Covid-19 have only reinforced and metastasised this profound violation.

If corporate shareholders were a proxy for society or societal welfare as a whole, inequalities in share ownership would matter less or violate fewer principles of justice. But this is not the case. Despite claims of the broadening distribution of financial wealth, Anglo-American economies are far removed from the utopia of a 'shareholder democracy' promised by Margaret Thatcher. In 2021, new analysis by the Federal Reserve found the wealthiest 10 percent of Americans owned 89 percent of stocks and mutual funds, with stark disparities in financial wealth between white, Black, and Hispanic households.[27] The UK is only marginally less extreme. Rhetorical commitment to a share-holding 'democracy' has given way to the reality of consolidated wealth holdings: the richest 1 percent own 39 percent of total direct share-based wealth, more than the poorest 90 percent combined.[28] While some might argue that private pension wealth is growing and becoming more dispersed, it remains strikingly unequal. The wealthiest 10 percent own an estimated 54 percent of American pension entitlements; the bottom half only 3.1 percent.[29] In the UK, the richest 20 percent of households by income own almost half of the country's pension wealth.[30] And because these assets accrue to individuals over their lifetimes, older pension holders' interests are disproportionately represented, and perhaps even in conflict with those of younger cohorts. In short, the interests of the invested wealth of a minority are hardly guaranteed to be a reflection of the majority. Moreover, pensions are not like financial wealth. They cannot be liquidated at will; they are deferred wages – a smaller paycheck today in exchange for a secure income in retirement. Few workers benefit from a deal that offers worsening wages and conditions in their working lives so as to benefit wealth-holders today, for the distant and unlikely promise of surging real-term gains in retirement based on asset ownership. Perhaps most fundamentally of all, in an economy in which assets are central yet highly unequally owned, negative externalities for society as a whole can very easily become a positive outcome for those at the top of the pyramid. Imagine, for example, an economy in which shareholders of listed firms reap the largest share of productivity gains while real wages for workers stagnate – a good description of Anglo-capitalist societies in recent decades. In that economy, corporate actions with negative externalities for society as a whole may well be perceived as a positive externality for those near the top of the wealth distribution.

How Ownership Drives Exploitation and Expropriation

Dynamics of ownership – dispossession, concentration, dependency – set in train the locomotive force of capitalism as a social relationship and economic system. As Marx famously argued, within capitalism we are free in two senses. Capitalism is premised on the freedom to sell our labour in exchange for a wage on the labour market. But through processes of enclosure, we are also 'freed' from the means by which we could subsist without having to sell our labour power as a commodity. Without sufficient assets to leverage for our continued survival or access to the gifts of the commons, we are tethered to our jobs, even if some of us have some relative freedom to choose what that job may be, and how we might spend those wages that are left after

securing the necessities of survival. This asymmetrical freedom means those who only possess their labour power are
'like one who is bringing his own hide to market and has
nothing to expect but – a hiding'.[31]

The asymmetry of resources and bargaining power
between labour and capital means what at first appears to
be a fair exchange between the worker and the employer is
in fact a contract for legalised economic exploitation: under
capitalism waged labour is by definition paid less than the
value it produces, with the surplus accruing to the capitalist – for example, senior management or shareholders – who
is then free to reinvest the surplus for their benefit. The
unfreedom and inequality at the heart of wage labour is
thus not the product of some inherent immorality of individuals but rather the unidirectional force of the system:
the worker cannot claim the wealth they produce under
capitalism because if they did, it would cease to function
as a system, premised as it is on the growth of capital and
accumulation. Ownership, by creating the conditions of
market dependency; disproportionately siphoning off the
surplus towards capital from labour; and concentrating coordinating power in the hands of capital owners, is constitutive
of this hierarchy.[32]

This exploitation is undergirded by two essential processes: enclosure and expropriation.[33] Property rights (often
unjustly imposed) confer on certain individuals and organisations prioritised access and use of resources, allowing
them to appropriate huge quantities of what Jason W.
Moore and Raj Patel call 'cheap natures', those things made
actively cheap (nature, money, work, care, food, energy,
and lives) and available in the world for expropriation.[34]
Expropriation takes many forms:[35] directly, from wage-labour

in production, but also in the (ongoing) violent dispossession of the land of Indigenous peoples to the hyper-modern land and resource grabs underlying the commodity sectors;[36] from the violent accumulation of New World slavery and genocidal conquest to the forms of bondage that suffuse informal employment and global supply chains; from the looting and legalised theft of the resources of the periphery by the capitalist centres, to colonial dispossesion and corporate asset-grabbing. This was and is a process of plunder on a world-transforming scale in which wealth is condensed into and through unequal property claims. In short, the appropriation of the wealth of others is not an unintended side effect, but the whole point. As Walter Rodney summarised in his seminal work, *How Europe Underdeveloped Africa*, 'The acquisition of wealth is not due to hard work alone, or the Africans working as slaves in America and the West Indies would have been the wealthiest group in the world. The individualism of the capitalist must be seen against the hard and unrewarded work of the masses.'[37] Importantly, the seizure of the 'free gifts of nature'[38] goes hand in hand with the mobilisation of the work of social reproduction (in effect the work of the home, from childcare to cooking and all manner of unpaid tasks) to drive capital accumulation, giving capitalism its gendered and racialised character.[39] Throughout the pandemic these tendencies were strongly reinforced, not least with children staying home from school adding further social reproduction to the work of wage labouring. Contemporary expropriation also increasingly revolves around the question of who issues and controls debt. Unequal ownership of government debt, for example, transfers money from ordinary taxpayers to bondholders as governments pay interest from elevated borrowing in lieu of higher taxation, a political choice to prioritise financial asset owners.[40] Meanwhile, extortionate rates on consumer credit and overdrafts redistribute money from individuals struggling on stagnant wages to creditors.[41] This financial expropriation became particularly pronounced during the pandemic, from the acute and devastating monetary constraints imposed on governments of the Global South, to indebted households struggling to stay afloat on suspended incomes, to the surge in predatory acquisitions of distressed businesses by private equity firms.

The imperative to expropriate in order to sustain itself means that capitalism is and has always been racially unequal in character.[42] Too often overlooked as the casualties of the 2008 financial crash, for example, the predatory extension of unsustainably expensive 'subprime' mortgages – 'disproportionately perpetrated against the poor and communities of color'[43] and packaged into tidy financial securities for yield-hungry investors – was borne out of finance's drive to expand its horizons for expropriation. In the end it was not financiers who lost it all, but these same families whose homes were repossessed and whose security evaporated, and who – more than a decade later – are still paying disproportionately for a crisis they didn't create.[44]

Expropriation also extends the ability to extract wealth beyond the classical exploitation of market-based wage labour into the unequal division of the impacts of ecological crisis.[45] Property relations enable firms to designate certain lands and people 'zones of sacrifice' to serve the demands for resources and 'sinks' that sustain the everyday life of the global affluent, from mining sites devastating local ecology to land seizure for carbon offsets.[46] Ownership claims – acting as a vehicle for normalising expropriation – have in this way been central to the construction of racial capitalism, acting as the fulcrum between the 'mutually constitutive' dynamics of economic exploitation and racial oppression.[47] The legal codes and property forms that divide and order economic and social life based on exclusive ownership are what enable capitalism to assign differential value to human and non-human lives, communities, ecosystems, and forms of labour. The time is long overdue for their remaking.

2

The Primacy of Property

The standard of living of the average American has to decline.
— Paul Volcker, former chairman of the
Federal Reserve, 1979[1]

*We do need to see a moderation of wage rises, now that's pain-
ful. I don't want to in any sense sugar that, it is painful.*
— Andrew Bailey, governor of the
Bank of England, February 2022

Our economic system is one which centres the interests of
private property. There is nothing organic or inevitable about
this arrangement. It has been cemented by a successful and
carefully articulated poli tical project: neoliberalism. Neoliberalism is a political project whose founding goal was to
make the world safe, free and profitable for property. Neoliberal actors, over time and space, have sought to protect
property from democratic demands and redistributional
pressures, and in doing so restore property's central role as
an organising force in the economy.[2] In the decades following
the Second World War, the sharply declining dynamism of
the advanced-capitalist world and the rising militancy and

ambition of post-colonial states, worker movements, and social coalitions struggling for a world transformed were, to the architects of neoliberalism, direct threats to the prerogatives of property and the goals of profit and growth.[3] Its emissaries – Margaret Thatcher and Ronald Reagan were most salient, but there were others before them – enacted sweeping reforms as a reaction to the erosion of capital's power and profitability in the 1970s. The programme buoyed the power of private ownership, breaking decisively with the constraints imposed on capital that had been won by organised labour and the redistributive political movements of the post-war era.

There was no guarantee this counter-revolution would succeed, of course. The Left was confident, and the working class comparatively organised. Old hierarchies of power and status were being challenged everywhere, from the household to the factory floor. These challenges could have been resolved through the extension, not the retrenchment, of democracy. Against this possibility, however, an emergent neoliberal movement moved to protect and extend the rights of capital and to halt the erosion of the wealth of asset holders through inflation. The 'economy' was to be shielded from democratic intervention. Over time, a range of neoliberal actors, from jurists and politicians to corporate interests and international organisations, have encased property relations within legal protections, safeguarding them against the threat of a more democratically accountable ownership regime.[4] Contrary to the popular perception of neoliberalism, then, this was never a project that sought to roll back the state. Instead, it sought to harness and, often, expand state power to enforce market relations.[5] The architects of neoliberalism emphasised the desirability and efficiency of 'the market' as the governing mode of social life and sought to inoculate economic goals against the dangerous spontaneity and unruly passion of political life. Yet they were also sceptical of the idea that market relations would emerge organically. Instead, the neoliberal era has been marked by consistent, coercive efforts to use state power to create and maintain a particular vision of a ubiquitous market society – finance-dominated, competitive, with technocracy dominant over politics – by extending private ownership and protecting property from egalitarian demands.[6]

The Deflationary Coalition

The mantra of this counter-revolution was simple: 'Stabilise prices, crush labour, discipline the South'.[7] It was driven by the aggressive and coordinated deployment of fiscal, monetary, and legal tools to reassert the rights of capital, overcome the perceived inefficiencies of planning relative to market forces, and eliminate the threat of organised labour. Privatisation was an essential tool in this respect. Selling off national infrastructure and assets for below-market rates, including housing, natural resources, railways, and utilities, transferred public wealth into private hands on a vast scale; fragmented and internationalised 'national economies' for the benefit of global investors and weakened state capacity, creating the self-reinforcing perception of a state less capable than the private sector.

The economic hierarchy created by this new arrangement, putting assets and asset owners first, was not just about redistributing ownership upwards through the privatisation of public wealth. A conjoined and critical goal was to implement a macro-political agenda that used fiscal and monetary policy to create favourable conditions for capital while breaking the power of labour and those living in the global 'peripheries', on whose resources, from cheap labour to raw materials, capitalist centres increasingly relied. The 'Volcker Shock'[8] – wherein the Fed aggressively increased interest rates as a tool in 1979–80 to induce a crushing recession and in doing so suppress inflation *and* traumatise the working class and indebted Global South – was the foundational event of this new world as much as the inter-related efforts to privatise public assets and expand the role and rights of private property ownership.[9] The regulation of inflation is always a political struggle over the distribution of the social surplus. The Volcker Shock was totemic in this sense, ushering in an era that decisively favoured wealthy asset owners over ordinary wage-earners and tamed inflation by lowering living standards. As the Bank of England governor Andrew Bailey's comments in our epigraph attest, that same instinct is alive and well today: a crisis not of their making will be resolved through an attack on the quality of life of ordinary people to protect the wealth and position of rich asset owners.

Driving and then sustaining the switch in inflationary regimes – from a world defined by wage inflation and asset-price stability, to wage stagnation and runaway asset-price inflation – was one of the signature achievements of the neoliberal turn. The result was to transfer wealth and income from labour to capital on a historic scale.[10] Central to the endurance of this new consensus was the mobilisation of what political economist Yakov Feygin has termed 'the deflationary bloc', an electoral and economic coalition that united ordinary (and often new, thanks to strategic policies such as Right to Buy) homeowners, small-scale business owners, and the asset rich in pursuit of policies that protected and inflated their wealth, whether in real estate or financial assets, relative to wage-earners.[11] The shift from defined benefit to defined contribution pensions – which made income dependent on financial market performance – augmented this. A new growth regime resulted, one that was returns-led rather than wage-driven, focused on maintaining the health of asset owners, and heavily reliant on debt-financed consumption over productive investment. Over time, the combination of new patterns of asset ownership (including broad-based home ownership), rapid inflation of the value of these assets, and the entrenched stagnation of wages created new dynamics of inequality that reshaped notions of class and social position.[12] In the process, this created complex electoral cleavages: in the UK, for example, recent Conservative electoral dominance has rested not so much on the party's appeal to the new working class, as on its domination of a heterogeneous asset-owning bloc.[13]

Unlike the post-war settlement preceding it, which benefited from an expanding mass market based on rising real wages and strong aggregate demand growth, neoliberalism was thus not particularly interested in wage growth – nor indeed in the disruptive effects of economic dynamism. Sustained strong growth risked causing inflationary pressure, likely triggering an increase in real interest rates that in turn would depress asset prices and increase the cost of borrowing, therefore harming the interests of key elements of this nascent political coalition, not least increasingly indebted homeowners and over-leveraged corporate actors. A low-pressure economy was not a sign of failure: better a slow-growing economy where capital rules and asset prices rise than a buoyant economy where labour is strong and power contested. Compounding this, the inability to replace manufacturing as the engine of growth in deindustrialising capitalist centres meant the post-'79 cycle of accumulation was defined by slowdown. Virtually every standard indicator – output, investment, employment, and wages – continued, with brief unsustained exceptions, their decade by decade, business cycle by business cycle deterioration.[14]

Traumatic as this experience was for many working communities, critically, profitability was revived. The active restructuring of the international economy away from manufacturing and towards finance under the wing of American power and the ongoing rentierisation of Anglo-capitalist societies increased the profitability of the overall economy,[15] while doing little to address the deeper source of capitalism's slowdown. Through this, capital's share of income in advanced economies grew tremendously at the expense of labour, consolidating the power of a wealthy ownership class who appropriated the lion's share of the gains, and cementing a new and expanded political coalition. In doing so, the neoliberal movement succeeded in restructuring the global economy in favour of asset-holders, thereby installing (in conjunction with the collapse of the Bretton Woods agreement in the early 1970s) the explosive growth of finance as the central driver of the Anglo-American economies.

The expansive, open-ended quality of an increasingly finance-led, asset-dominated global economy created a world in which, as Martijn Konings has written, 'what really mattered was the possibility of keeping the system going, from one day to the next, above all keeping afloat those entities that could drag the whole system down with them'.[16] Economic actors, whether corporations or households, became increasingly oriented towards generating sufficient cash flow to service their rising indebtedness, with power consequently flowing to the institutions that could generate credit and liquidity: corporations, the financial sector, and above all central banks. In this new world, the explosive growth of finance was not (and is not) a bubble bound to burst. Rather, it is a growth whose sustainability is dependent on political intervention and access to credit, rather than underlying attributes of the 'real economy'.[17] This access is predicated on ownership – for households, access to loans is supported by ownership of assets for collateral, such as a car or savings account; for corporations, the cost of borrowing is significantly influenced by the health of their balance sheet – in other words, their ownership of assets. Consider that we have had two economic heart attacks in the span of a decade: the 2008 financial crash, and the financial mayhem that ensued from the initial shock of the pandemic. In both cases, the centrality of asset owners and their interests (that is, high and rising asset prices) meant that central banks stood ready with the defibrillator, ensuring those interests were secured rather than letting the bubbles burst.

The Rise of the Rentier

As a result of these processes, Anglo-American capitalist economies are now defined by 'rent'. Rent, as the geographer Brett Christophers argues, is 'income derived from the ownership, possession or control of scarce assets under conditions of limited or no competition', in contrast to production-based income within a competitive market. 'Rentier capitalism' thus describes an economy structured around the ownership of key types of assets and the income streams they generate, and by extension around those who own them.[18] Christophers points to seven main asset classes that constitute the core of rentier capitalism: land and property (both residential and commercial); financial assets and the creditor-debtor relationship; intellectual property assets such as patents and copyrights; natural resources, such as hydrocarbons and metal commodities; digital platforms like Facebook; service contracts, such as for outsourcing; and the privatised utilities sector, including telecommunication, energy, transportation, and similar services. Together, these sectors form the nucleus of rentier economies, for which rent-seeking through concentrated ownership is no longer fringe but the beating heart.

On its own narrow terms, rentierism has worked, at least for its asset-owning beneficiaries. Profits have been restored, shareholder wealth enlarged, and wealth previously held by the public or belonging to the commons made available for private ownership and use. Contemporary forms of rentierism are centred around sweating assets instead of investment to create new value – in other words, it is 'less about *making* anything and more about simply *owning* something'.[19] Though this is a fundamentally property-driven ethos, rather than an entrepreneurial one, we should carefully avoid the temptation to establish a false dichotomy between a non-extractive 'productive capitalism' of justly earned corporate income, and the unearned spoils of extractive 'rentier capitalism'. The extraction of value from labour and nature and the mesh of unremunerated activities and resources that sustain the economy remain fundamental to those profits; in other words, due to its underlying patterns of ownership, all of capitalism is in some fundamental sense about rent and the cornering of economic power through property.[20] However, the pronounced turn towards rent-seeking in terms of the locus of power and profit within our societies has been key to reasserting the primacy of property, making asset ownership more fundamental than ever.

While rentierism has not managed to resolve the economic issues that underlie stagnation,[21] politically it has proven a success. Financialisation and rentierisation have created a mesh of asset ownership through the global economy that is now far more complex than simply 'the 1 percent versus the rest', even as it has led to an explosion in wealth at the very top. Most obviously, it has been translated into the widespread, politically facilitated increase in home ownership, which increasingly defines shifting class boundaries and political leanings.[22] The structure of the economy and present electoral coalitions in advanced economies have been reshaped by this logic. Moreover, the extension of private pension coverage and other forms of saving means many working people now have stronger ties to the relentless rise of public company share prices and financial markets than in the past, even if the feeling of entanglement is often much stronger than its actual effects on the majority's financial well-being. In the UK, for example, when surging energy prices in early 2022 led to calls for a windfall tax on oil majors' record profits, many detractors argued – incorrectly – that this would represent a tax on ordinary UK pensioners. In reality, UK pension funds collectively hold a dwindling stake in major listed companies like Shell or BP,[23] and their hugely diversified portfolios would make this impact negligible, while creating a means for reducing immediate and acute suffering, most saliently among pensioners who are disproportionately affected by fuel poverty.

Nonetheless, the argument against the tax packs an emotional and rhetorical punch that has, at the time of writing, proven difficult to overcome. This entanglement – and the surging value of assets like real estate that are a lifeline for many ordinary people – has made it more difficult to build a political coalition strong enough to challenge rentier power, even as the need for deep reform – including, ironically, with respect to providing security and dignity in old age without relying on financial markets – has become more urgent.

A Crisis of Balance Sheets

In the wake of the 2008 financial crisis, government and central bank interventions repeated an old pattern, whereby losses were socialised while gains were privatised on an unprecedented scale. In the US alone, the direct cost of bailouts for major corporations was almost $500 billion. As unjust as these outcomes were, the processes revealed the contradictory and potentially transformative potential contained within existing political-economic arrangements: the market-ordering and planning function of central banks, alongside their ability to conjure liquidity at will, was underscored; the reliance of private wealth on public resources was driven powerfully home; and small if important steps forward were taken in the regulation of 'too big to fail' firms and the plumbing of international finance. The seeds of a progressive response – namely mobilising public financial power to reorder the economy and embracing democratic planning – were visible. Perhaps above all, it was a reminder of Walter Benjamin's assertion, 'The experience of our generation: capitalism will not die of natural causes'.

The lesson, however, was not heeded, and the transitional strategies to recover and transcend the institutional structures that gave rise to the crisis were not taken. Instead, macro-political tools were deployed, above all quantitative easing (QE = massive central bank purchases of government and corporate bonds) and austerity, to keep the status quo on life support. As ordinary households endured a decade of austerity, with growing insecurity and stagnant real income growth, and the global economy stuttered through a historically sluggish recovery held back by weak demand and anaemic investment, the stock market surged. The S&P 500 grew by 190 percent over the decade, and real estate valuations on both sides of the Atlantic broke record after record. This was an unprecedented bull run for owners of corporate financial wealth. Even as many communities struggled to recover from a recession they had no role in creating, the S&P 500 Total Return Index gained 13.4 percent per annum against a historic average of 9.7 percent.[24] In the UK, 2019 saw dividend payments from the FTSE 100 hit a record high of £110.5 billion, ending a decade in which workers had suffered the longest pay squeeze since Napoleon's armies were fighting to restore slavery in Haiti. This capped a decade in which the 100 largest UK-based non-financial companies paid out over £400bn in dividends – the equivalent of 68% of their net profits over 2011–18.[25] The economic and geopolitical aftershocks of the crisis, and the decisions made in its wake, continue to decisively reshape and destabilise our politics.

The extraordinary decoupling of returns to wage-earners compared with asset owners was the result of political decision-making, not abstract 'market forces'. With fiscal policy acting as a brake on recovery in the 2010s (bar China's historic post-crisis stimulus), central banks were entrusted with reviving the global economy. Their response was to turn the supposedly temporary measure of quantitative easing into a permanent feature of monetary policy, showering markets with ultra-cheap credit. By extending and deepening their asset purchasing programme, the balance sheets of the world's largest central banks – the Fed, Bank of Japan, PBOC, and the ECB – expanded spectacularly over the decade, from roughly $5 trillion in 2007 to $20 trillion just before the pandemic began, spiking again to almost $30 trillion over the course of 2020–21.[26] The Bank of England's programme of asset purchases saw a similar explosion in the size of its balance sheet growth. By holding interest rates at the floor and reducing the yield on government bonds even into negative real terms (meaning lenders were effectively paying for the privilege of parking their cash with the government), central banks encouraged income-seeking investors to pour money into stocks and real estate. The idea was that reducing the cost of borrowing, easing funding conditions, and stimulating asset prices[27] would be enough to trigger a sustained increase in corporate investment and boost consumption, driving a durable recovery.

Through the Looking Glass

Instead, while monetary policy supercharged asset prices, fiscal austerity held back the recovery and ushered in a historically anaemic decade, with many economies operating well below their productive potential throughout the 2010s. At the same time, there was a rapid shift towards market-based finance over traditional bank lending after 2008, with debt securities (bonds) assuming an increasingly central role in the international financial system. After a decade of monetary intervention in the form of QE, the financial system appeared to be through the looking glass: as the Fed pushed short-term interest rates to near 0 percent, other central banks went even further, taking the extraordinary step of introducing negative rates. By August 2019, the total value of bonds with negative yields climbed as high as $17 trillion, a symptom of a global economy whose loss of dynamism was upending assumed economic certainties.

These processes accelerated the ongoing mutation of advanced economies away from a starry-eyed popular if unrepresentative image of free market competition towards the reality of increasingly fused states and corporate economies. Even if the vision of competitive dynamism was always a kind of fiction, after 2008 the veil was brutally pulled back. What was left was something that perversely resembled the political Right's vision of dystopian statism: inequality amid stagnation, pervasive monopoly power, innovation dependent on the state's largesse, an oligarchic elite detached from the public at large and seemingly immune from democratic control, centralised authority in charge of decisions that decisively shaped everyday life, unaccountable institutions of economic planning, and the interweaving of public and private power.

Under these conditions many large corporations managed to accumulate vast piles of cash. Apple's Braeburn Capital, for example, which handles most of Apple's cash and short- and long-term securities, managed almost $270 billion in 2017, with its total liquid financial assets higher than the stock of foreign reserves of countries like Germany, the United Kingdom, and France.[28] Despite being flush with cash, corporations still took advantage of ultra-low interest rates to embark on a borrowing spree, with US corporate debt increasing 116 percent over the decade to a record high $7.1 trillion.[29] Importantly, this borrowing has often served less to finance investment than to reward shareholders, with many companies using the debt to buy back their own stock, redistributing wealth to their external investors while inflating the all-important 'earnings per share' metric – and in the process, the 'performance' of executives. In the opening quarter of 2019 alone, S&P 500 net repurchases climbed to an extraordinary $753 billion.[30] For 2019 as a whole, breaking down use of cash by S&P 500 companies, only 27 percent and 11 percent was spent on capital expenditure and R&D respectively; by contrast buybacks and dividends accounted for 29 percent and 18 percent.[31]

In terms of Anglo-American economies, then, the 2010s was a decade in which the soaring value of and payouts from financial assets split entirely from any corresponding growth in wages or other meaningful indicators of well-being like reduced poverty or decreased inequality. The result was an anaemic and unequal recovery sustained by the drip feed of QE and cheap debt to the benefit of large-scale owners of financial assets, rather than the public good. This was a low and dishonest decade. But even here, there is a kernel of hope in the experience. These outcomes were not inevitably generated by some unchangeable economic laws; as ever, they were the direct product of political choices and institutions oriented towards a narrow set of interests, all of which we have made and can remake.

Covid Capitalism

Whereas in 2008 the crisis moved from the financial markets into the real economy and saw private indebtedness transferred onto public sector balance sheets, the pandemic worked in reverse order.[32] As economies were demobilised, the shock was severe. Equity prices plummeted, capital flowed out of low-income economies at record rates, inducing sharp economic pain, and even the US Treasury market, the sturdy backbone and safe haven of global finance, hit turbulence. With financial markets in freefall and the global economy lurching into a historic downturn, on 23 March 2020 the US Federal Reserve declared that it would 'do whatever it takes' to avert a global depression. It was true to its word. The range and scale of interventions was unprecedented: cutting its target for the federal funds rate, the rate banks pay to borrow from each other overnight; undertaking a massive and ongoing securities purchasing programme worth trillions of dollars; offering low-cost loans to corporations; backstopping money market mutual funds, and more.[33] Acting in concert with the world's central banks and treasuries, this swift, historic set of actions averted meltdown. Markets were stabilised but the unequal pattern of public backstopping of private gains was repeated.

And gains there were. The intervention triggered an explosive divergence in economic fortunes between the performance of financial assets and the experience of everyday workers and communities. As whole economies demobilised, stock markets – in freefall as the pandemic began – surged spectacularly. As of May 2021, the S&P 500 was up 29 percent from 1 January 2020, and the first half of 2021 was the best six months for global stock markets in nearly four decades. With corporate equity ownership concentrated among the wealthiest, the result was a staggering, politically mediated increase in inequality. In a year in which between 200 and 500 million people were forced into extreme poverty, the world's billionaires added $5 trillion to their wealth, the fastest surge in a decade.[34]

Yet, as dire as the pandemic and its economic fallout have been, it has been ripe with transformative potential. Unparalleled coordination between fiscal and monetary authorities has enabled an extraordinary and sustainable expansion in public spending during the crisis. For example, the scale of the Bank of England's bond-buying programme meant even though the UK government's borrowing increased by £303 billion in the financial year 2020–21, the cost of servicing that debt *fell* from £48 billion to £38 billion. Indeed, the aggregate cost of servicing UK debt hit historical lows. This is not an aberration – debt servicing costs have been falling across all advanced economies since the 1980s,[35] and higher public borrowing does not necessarily imply higher public borrowing *costs*. With the Bank of England owning a vast proportion of the UK's public debt, the power to influence debt servicing costs – and act to keep debt servicing costs sustainable – is firmly in the hands of public institutions.

All of this opens up a tantalising historical parallel: if the Volcker Shock helped usher in the era of asset owners, monetary policy could redeem itself by helping enable a sustainable, transformative step change in public spending to anchor a recovery centred on meeting urgent social and ecological needs. Nor is the UK alone; the crisis has reconfirmed in striking fashion the expansive power certain privileged states retain when fiscal and monetary institutions are free to, and do, act in lockstep. Critically, even here there is the enclosure of privilege, with the same fiscal and monetary freedoms denied to the majority of the world's governments, who are forced to borrow on global markets at heavy cost, both with respect to interest rates and insecurity. If this continues unchanged, swathes of the global population will continue to be held hostage to the return profiles demanded by private investors, which will compromise their ability to invest in urgent needs, from public health to climate adaptation.

The first test is already here. With the easing of lockdown set to be followed by an economic boom and transitional inflationary pressure, the forces of the deflationary bloc are mobilising, insisting that the maintenance of price stability should be the key policy goal. Calls for aggressive interest rate hikes – hailing from positions of significant influence[36] – are code for maintaining labour's weakness and protecting the interests of asset owners. Inflation always has a range of 'winners' and 'losers'; it typically disadvantages the holders of large-scale financial wealth while relatively benefiting debtors and people whose main source of income is wages and inflation-indexed benefits. A deflationary strategy therefore worsens inequalities by design, given existing disparities in wealth and income. Instead of heeding these false warnings, we should (regrettably) take a page from the playbook of the turbulent, politically enforced neoliberal transition of the 1980s: any serious break with the primacy of property will require strong nerves to confront the grip of asset ownership over the economy. If nerves hold, however, public power can be mobilised to build economies that centre life over property.

3

Engines of Extraction

On the face of it, shareholder value is the dumbest idea in the world.
— Jack Welch, former CEO of General Electric[1]

As economies across the world ground to a halt following lockdown orders, panic struck global financial markets. Even blue chip corporations began to sound the alarm on a coming wave of layoffs. In response, governments took unprecedented action, committing trillions of dollars worldwide in state-backed, no-strings-attached loan guarantees; implementing a set of facilities to purchase corporate debt, often irrespective of the debt's rating; and undertaking a suite of direct bailouts. In the UK, the Treasury's 'Covid Corporate Financing Facility', in concert with the Bank of England, provided special-access loan negotiations to only the largest corporations, while in the US, over $2 trillion in government grants and loans were dished out to businesses which generally weren't required to prove their need, or even commit to retaining employees.[2]

The results were predictable. The largest corporations, often sitting on huge stockpiles of cash, weathered the storm, while small businesses collapsed by the tens of thousands, and private equity firms hoovered up distressed assets. US unemployment reached its highest rate since the Second World War. However, for shareholders the pandemic's economic impact looked quite different. Many corporations were given quick access to credit without stipulations on how it should be used. In the UK, discount airliner EasyJet was able to gorge on a £600 million public and favourably termed loan while paying out over £170 million in dividends in 2020, including £60 million to its founder. This was only one such example; central bank interventions that kept interest rates at record lows coalesced with a lockdown-induced savings glut among the wealthy into a blockbuster year for the stock markets. The assets under management of BlackRock and Vanguard, the world's foremost asset management firms, swelled to unprecedented highs, nearing $20 trillion at the time of writing, with vast ownership stakes in every sector. BlackRock CEO Larry Fink's 2020 remuneration was $30 million, a stunning 18 percent raise over the previous year.[3] For many, the sheer scale of disconnect between the Wall Street boom and the tragic reality on the ground left deep cracks in the already tenuous notion that the stock market reflects the real economy.

A year into the pandemic, the absurd spectacle of the r/WallStreetBets phenomenon helped crumble that façade even further. Users of the website Reddit piled into the stock market in order to drive up the share price of Game-Stop, the US-based computer game store, in the hope of bankrupting hedge funds holding significant 'short' positions in the retailer's stock ('shorting' being, in effect, a bet on the decline in a stock's price). The spectacle exploded on social media, drawing responses that ranged from triumphant cheers to horrified outrage and, admittedly, a great deal of confusion surrounding the financial machinations underlying it all. Best of all were the stern admonishments from those who, while 'sympathising' with the Robin Hood stylings of the GameStop 'vigilantes', nonetheless scolded them for their recklessness. A columnist for *Business Insider*, for instance, wrote on Twitter: 'I know people think this is fun but – why do we have a stock market? So productive firms can raise capital to do useful things. Detaching stock price from fundamental value makes the markets serve the real economy worse.'[4]

Earnest as this appeal may have been, it's fundamentally misrepresentative – and revealing proof of the extent to which the interests of shareholders have, in the common sense, become synonymous with the interests of society writ large. Stock prices have been divorced from even the market's indicators of 'fundamental value' for years, with central bank asset purchase programmes in the wake of the 2008 financial crisis heavily inflating asset prices. More importantly, most of what happens on the stock market is not 'raising productive capital' for investment in the things most of us would consider valuable – higher wages, decarbonisation and sustainable production, increased productivity to expand leisure time, supply chain justice, or investment in R&D that meets urgent needs. The extent to which companies issue new shares to raise funds is dwarfed by the rate of corporate buyouts and share buybacks; in other words, much more cash flows out of firms to shareholders than the reverse.[5] Rather than raising capital, the contemporary stock market is – and has long been – a remarkably effective tool for repatterning ownership claims on economic output and, in doing so, for concentrating wealth and economic power.[6]

By providing a route for capital to phase-shift from fixed to liquid, turning 'a concrete claim on a particular production process into an abstract claim on the social product in general', and allowing the extraction of rent from production towards the ownership class, the function of the stock markets is clear: 'to give capitalists their exit'.[7] The structural power of finance depends upon the preservation of market liquidity, which the stock market provides. As J. W. Mason writes: 'Their ability to get rid of assets at any time allows the owners of financial assets to discipline states and constrain firms to disgorge cash to their shareholders.'[8]

So while the r/WallStreetBets army may have nearly toppled a hedge fund, they scarcely rocked the structures of capital itself. Indeed, in forcing their target, Melvin Capital, to break a sweat, they inadvertently created a boon for other shareholders in GameStop (and for another hedge fund linked to the ownership of the share trading platform Robinhood that was used for the assault).[9] The decisive intervention from Robinhood to freeze trading of GameStop on its platform reflected the true balance of power in this modern David and Goliath. The battle was fought entirely on the terms of those with assets to protect – the same terms that structured states' swift and sweeping support for corporations and financial markets as the pandemic struck, bailing out corporations and asset owners even as jobs were shed at breakneck pace and the global ranks of the extreme poor swelled by the hundreds of millions.[10] The contours of the pandemic, and of our responses to systemic challenges like the climate crisis, cannot be understood without clearly charting these terms – the systems, institutions, and logics enveloping the central institution around which capitalism is structured: the corporation.

The corporation – wielding extraordinary legal privileges to organise production for profit; acting with sovereign, world-shaping power; and functioning as a vehicle for the vast upward concentration of wealth – is at the heart of the many crises we face. It is also, in embryonic form, an institution of potential transformation. Made democratic and rescued from the disciplining force of financial markets, its immense power to coordinate production could be repurposed in service of meeting social and environmental needs and providing good, genuinely free forms of work. This dual quality makes the corporation a central question in both our ability to understand our converging, compounding crises, and in our collective ability to move beyond them.

It's the Corporation's World, We're All Just Living in It

We live in a corporate economy. Subject to the commandment 'grow or die!', the corporation organises entire swathes of our economy, commands vast resources, and exercises immense social and political power. Islands of non-market planning, with production organised through internal planning and vertical forms of coordination rather than the price mechanism and horizontal competition, their design and operation intimately shapes our lives, our communities, our ecologies. They are the terrain in which surplus value is generated by labour and appropriated by capital, and within it, capital has all the bargaining power, turning a notionally free exchange of employment contracts between equal parties into a contract for unequal distribution of the rewards. Despite rumours of its demise, the corporation still dominates global economic activity, accounting for the majority of gross value added in the OECD, with just the 5,000 largest firms enjoying $40 trillion in revenue in 2019.[11] While there are numerous other forms of enterprise, such as co-operatives, it is because of this enduring scale and world-making force that we focus here on the corporate form in particular. The vast and overlapping balance sheets of the largest multinational corporations are now of systemic importance, and their fragility triggered the unprecedented scale of state support provided in the spring of 2020. Indeed, as Hyun-Song Shin, head of research of the Bank of International Settlements – the central bank of central banks – argues, the global economy is best viewed not as a series of national 'islands' trading with each other, but a massive matrix of interlocking corporate balance sheets.[12]

The corporation is also a key site for the appropriation of the social product for the benefit of that central figure of the rentier economy: the shareholder. Unlike the majority of the population, whose claim to that product is exercised through wages in exchange for work, or via the household economy or public entitlements through residence, the shareholder's claims are generated by ownership. However, this does not make the shareholder, nor the individual capitalist, the owner of the means of production. Instead, they are overwhelmingly owned, in the words of economist Doug Henwood, 'not by natural persons, but by abstract legal entities – corporations'.[13]

Through the invention of share capital, the corporation became able to capitalise the future, as the creation of tradable shares generated claims on the company's future earnings, which in turn began to be speculatively traded on rapidly growing stock markets. Shareholders asserted their claims on the productive force of the corporation through their ownership of this new form of financial property, with shareholders' entitlements based on their being 'residual claimants' – in theory, the primary risk-takers of the corporation, with no guarantees of a return. As a result, the corporation became a portal for organising financial flows between the past, present, and future for the enrichment of its shareholders.

Though the corporation today exists as an icon of private wealth and market dynamics, the corporate form is neither private nor the product of spontaneous market ordering. On the contrary, the corporation is a creation of legal fiat; its authority, privileges, and powers are all publicly granted. The corporation is constituted by law;[14] maintained by political effort; and often directly supported by public money, as the raft of bailouts over recent decades remind us. Consequently, it is subject to public contestation and democratic reordering. The original public–private partnership, the corporation can – and must – be remade.

A History of Violence

The modern business corporation emerged in lockstep with the violence of European colonialism. The earliest corporations, such as the British East India Company, were individually chartered through unique Acts of Parliament. From birth, the corporate form was thus a state–private partnership as well as a central institution of colonial expansion. These companies were privileged with rights and powers that enabled them to organise acts of dispossession, violence, coercion, and environmental devastation for the enrichment of financial asset holders, processes that remain one of the corporation's key signatures.

The law and its corollary, the threat of coercive enforcement, were the tools that set the corporate form in motion.
Though there are many different business forms with diverse
ownership structures, the corporation came to dominate
through its particular combination of legal privileges and
property rights. Endowed with legal personhood (rights
comparable to those of a person) in 'a bizarre – even farcical – series of lawsuits more than 130 years ago' in the early
American judiciary,[15] the corporation became entitled to
own assets in its own name, command labour, and coordinate economic activity at scale. In the United States, the
Citizens United case protected corporations' 'freedom of
speech' by legally forbidding legislation to limit corporate
political donations under the First Amendment. Thus, while
the 'firm' is the economic organisation of the business – an
entity of complex, intensely political relationships of
command and hierarchy – the firm, in turn, is ruled by the
legal structure of the corporation. The advent of limited
shareholder liability, meanwhile, transferred risk from the
shareholder to the corporation's employees, creditors, and
the state – a privilege still fulsomely enjoyed today. In the
case of a bankruptcy, limited liability protects shareholders,
guaranteeing that, at worst, they will lose the value of their
share capital, leaving the company's workers and the public
to pick up the rest of the tab. Despite this shift in liability,
control rights over a corporation's strategic direction have
become synonymous with ownership, suggesting the public
corporation is a dominion of private power.

The manner in which the corporation is governed still
bears the imprint of its origins in an era where the vast
majority of humanity were disenfranchised economically
and politically. The government of the corporation, which

sets the direction of the firm, organises its purpose, and allocates its surplus, is, in Anglo-American capitalism, the exclusive domain of capital. Investors control the government of the corporation, with the company's executive (its board) appointed by its legislature (the shareholder body). Labour is (in the vast majority of cases) entirely excluded from governance despite producing the corporation's wealth. Perversely, power is awarded to the parties that bear little risk and make little contribution and denied to those without whom the business would cease to function and whose livelihoods are most at risk if it fails. Moreover, the governance of the corporation is deeply undemocratic. Corporate voting power is not awarded on an equal basis among stakeholders subject to the corporation's rule but is instead allocated in direct proportion to ownership of a company's total share wealth. For the worker, then, the corporation is an undemocratic institution over which they have little control, even though much of their life is organised through its structures. This central institution of capitalism therefore stands in direct tension with democracy and justice.[16]

The Abolition of the Capitalist Mode of Production

Within a few decades of its birth, Marx had detected an emergent and profoundly radical possibility contained within the institutional design of the corporation: 'the abolition of the capitalist mode of production within the capitalist mode of production itself'.[17] In other words, as the economy became ever more complex and interdependent, Marx perceived a process at work eroding the claims of private property that could have emancipatory effect.[18] He argued that the corporation, the vanguard institution of capitalism, was also the system's coming gravedigger. Two shifts in corporate ownership were driving an explosive tension between the socialisation of production in the corporate form and the privatisation of its wealth through claims of ownership.

First, the growth of the modern corporation accelerated the separation of ownership and control. Whereas the capitalist had once been unified in a single figure – the owner-manager, at once the direct owner of the means of production and the manager of production – as the complexity and scale of corporate activity grew it encouraged the separation of the two essential functions of ownership and direction. This division between owners and managers represented an ongoing split – albeit a split within a single ongoing process of accumulation – between capital as property and capital as managerial function and social relationship, one overseeing production but without an ownership claim, the other an ownership class without direct control of the means of production.[19] The question is, if managers coordinated production and disciplined labour power, what role did the owner play? Superfluous from production, why did share ownership grant income and control rights?

Second, Marx recognised that the separation of ownership and control took place against the backdrop of the socialisation of property within the corporation itself. As the scale and cost of financing corporate activities grew, the growing capitalist credit system drove an enormous centralisation of existing firms and their capital.[20] While this pooling greatly improved access to credit, it also diluted the claim any one individual (or share) exercised over the corporation – all while legal changes over the course of the nineteenth century confirmed that it was the corporate body, *not the shareholder*, that owned the means of production.[21] Rather than controlling and directly owning a share of a tangible material asset like a factory, share ownership now implied passively possessing some intangible, depersonalised corporate capital – an entitlement to a share of future profits. This emergence of two distinct forms of property, one for shareholders that could be traded on financial markets and another for the corporation's assets, was to have critical implications.

In effect, individually owned property was replaced by socialised property pooled in the form of the corporation and stock markets, while private shareholders continued to set the purpose and appropriate the proceeds of socialised production. Disruptive as this process was, it was central to the extraordinary growth that capitalism unleashed. But it raised a dangerous question: If production is organised within the corporation and value is created by labour and nature, nowhere but in the act of accumulating wealth created by others does the share-owner appear. Why then should shareholders continue to be treated as 'owners' of the corporation, monopolising income and control rights? Marx was not alone in asking.

Functionless, Futureless?

In his 1926 essay, 'The End of Laissez Faire', John Maynard Keynes wrote: 'One of the most interesting and unnoticed developments of recent decades has been the tendency of big enterprise to socialise itself.' For Keynes, the pooling and anonymisation of ownership enabled by financial markets had seemingly severed the link between the shareholder and actual enterprise. It was through this process that the modern corporation – to borrow from the New

Deal corporate legal theorists Adolf Berle and Gardiner Means – 'dissolved the [private] property atom'.[22] There were now two forms of property: one active, the tangible assets owned by the corporation and controlled by the managers; the other passive, revenue rights owned by shareholders that were 'liquid, impersonal, and involving no responsibility'. In this context, Berle and Means argued, it made little sense either legally or morally to view shareholders as the owners of the corporation or enthrone their interests in its governance.[23] Instead, they argued corporations should expunge these claims – hangovers from an era when ownership and management were combined – and reorient production towards meeting collectively defined goals. This was the post-capitalist potential within a corporation turned upside down: with the expropriator expropriated, the redundant claim of the shareholder could be replaced by corporate forms that organised production under truly democratic direction and shared the social product among the true sources of wealth: labour and nature.

However, if Marx saw the corporation as the potential midwife for a post-capitalist mode of production, he also warned that trends in ownership and credit markets risked birthing a very different future: a new era of monopoly capitalism, dominated by finance. As it expanded and evolved, industrial capitalism followed this latter path, and the embryonic potential of the corporation to coordinate production and human innovation to generate good work and collective abundance was never fully realised. Instead, the industrial corporation became increasingly subordinated to finance, nurturing a wealthy cohort of owners who accrued rents through share ownership, mediated by a surging credit economy in a maelstrom of accumulation.

And surge, it did. The meteoric growth enabled by the corporate form depended on the concurrent expansion of financial markets. At the turn of the seventeenth century, in one of the earliest instances of transferrable claims on future income, the British and Dutch East India Companies issued shares to the general public which could be freely traded, to fund the brutal engines of imperialism.[24] Over time, the stock market as we now know it came of age with the modern corporation, becoming essential to the patterning of increasingly complex ownership claims within it. Despite this history and the shareholder's ongoing primacy in the ownership structure, today equity investment (creating new share capital) is not the limiting factor for corporate growth. Rather, the rates commanded by banks on their loans and investors in corporate bonds have fundamentally determined which types of enterprise gain access to capital based on the prospect for reward. And since, as economist Ann Pettifor writes, 'speculation can be much more lucrative in the short-term . . . many investors prefer the capital gains made from speculation', to the detriment of investment in productive, generative enterprise or, indeed, the not-for-profit undertakings that deliver so much value to society.[25]

The Truly Public Corporation?

In the decades either side of the Second World War, with global finance seemingly tamed by the Bretton Woods settlement and shareholders dispersed and relatively disempowered, 'managerial capitalism' – wherein managers represented the key agents of economic power – seemed entrenched. Among scholars of otherwise differing political beliefs, there was widespread agreement on the core thesis that decision-making power had passed definitively from shareholders to executives; that production, not financial claims against the productive process, was what mattered; and that managers, subject to social norms and controls, would prioritise the interests of the company.[26] Some social democratic 'modernisers' such as Tony Crosland argued that the new age of managerial control – to the relative detriment of the shareholder – heralded the end of the capitalist class as historically constituted. Fatefully, and fatally, this meant that attempts to reshape the corporation by dissolving dormant but still powerful shareholder rights fell by the wayside. While analyses such as Crosland's were clearly not borne out by reality, the insight that the managerial corporation did threaten the interests of the rent-seeking investor was correct. Within it, the shareholder was a relatively disempowered figure with limited collective influence, and the recipient of a sparse stream of modest dividends. Moreover, with business investment overwhelmingly funded out of internal earnings, stock markets ranked near the bottom in the hierarchy of finance. As a result, the corporation was relatively insulated from financial market pressure; absent this guiding force, it risked becoming an institution of planning to meet needs rather than an engine for enriching shareholders.[27]

Reversing this process was key to restoring the owner-rentiers' privileges. Beginning in the late 1960s, legislative, judicial, and managerial action on both sides of the Atlantic facilitated the rise of hostile takeovers,[28] corporate raiding, aggressive company restructuring, the revision of antitrust rules, the concentration of share ownership, and the growth of shareholder 'activism' – that is, shareholders' assertions of the primacy of their interests under threat of divestment.

The tenets of 'agency theory' emphasised the importance of the shareholder as a force against expropriation of corporate profits by 'insiders' – labour and management – giving ideological weight to the doctrine of shareholder primacy and value maximisation.[29]

This was not finance in aid of socially abundant production. Instead, financial and legal mechanisms were developed to ruthlessly refocus the corporation on the needs of the wealthy ownership class: maximising the share of corporate income distributed to investors. For the modern corporation in which the share price served as the ultimate barometer of performance – with a plunging stock leaving companies vulnerable to takeover – over time these new tools of financial discipline compelled corporations to turn over unprecedented levels of cash to shareholders.[30] Having remained fairly stable between 10 to 20 percent of cash flows in the 1960s and '70s, distribution to shareholders rose over the past several decades, peaking at 50 percent of total cash flows just before the 2008 financial crisis.[31] By another measure, between 2003 and 2012, the S&P 500 companies paid out an astonishing 91 percent of their earnings to shareholders – 37 percent in dividends and 54 percent in buybacks.[32] This dizzying U-turn in the corporation's priorities was not about efficiency but power, decisively remaking the corporation in the interests of capital.[33]

The prioritisation of shareholder interests occurred as part of the wider financialisation of the firm, though this remains a complex process. While it is undoubtedly true that the proportion of financial assets in the balance sheets of non-financial corporations have surged in recent decades, the proportion of financial asset-based *income* in non-financial firms remains relatively small; for example, in US non-financial corporations it averaged below 2.5 percent between the 1970s and 2017.[34] Thus, despite much commentary suggesting otherwise, companies still make their profits overwhelmingly in commodity production and sale, linked indelibly to the surplus value labour creates. However, the *distribution* of those earnings is now dominated by financial channels, not wages or reinvestment, with corporations' accumulation of financial assets carrying with it substantial tax benefits through the relative ease with which such assets and profits can be 'relocated' in low- or no-tax jurisdictions.[35]

This transition was a contingent, conflictual process, reflecting the malleability of the corporate form and the conflicts and relative power between the interests of different parties. The financialisation of the corporation was not simply externally imposed on management by activist shareholders; corporate managers were often eager co-participants in this shift,[36] recognising the utility of financial performance benchmarks for their interests, and happy to appropriate a share of the corporation's wealth for themselves.

The Great Reconcentration

For advocates of the new shareholder value regime, the argument was simple: corporations were owned by a vast number of diffuse shareholders who, having a singular interest in maximising their returns from the companies in which they were invested, would demand maximum corporate profitability. Profitability, in theory, should reflect superior productivity and efficiency, generating these socially beneficial outcomes as convenient by-products. And because they were comparatively weak, shareholders needed to be protected against 'expropriation' of their value by managers and workers.[37]

At the time the doctrine of shareholder value came to dominate, this argument was based broadly on real conditions. Most shareholders held very small stakes, perhaps a fraction of a percent, and their portfolios consisted of only a handful of companies whose performance (and payouts to shareholders) they were thus acutely interested in.[38] While significant inequalities in ownership of financial assets, particularly within an increasingly global economy, meant this was a far cry from the shareholder 'democracy' championed by Margaret Thatcher, at the very least the assumptions of the shareholder primacy doctrine reflected existing share ownership conditions at the time.

Fast forward to today, and the picture is strikingly different. Ownership of the global economy is dominated by a handful of financial behemoths: those asset managers who pool the assets of clients that range from wealthy individuals to multi-billion-dollar pension funds and, for a fee, invest these assets on their beneficiaries' behalf. Importantly, the transition to an asset manager–dominated system marks a further separation between ownership and control. While claims on future income remain with the ultimate owner of the asset (the, usually wealthy, individual), control rights associated with the legal act of shareholding are now overwhelmingly vested with an intermediary who legally owns the corporate shares.

The last few decades have seen a staggering reconcentration of share ownership within a few firms. At the time of writing, two American asset management titans – BlackRock and Vanguard – together control nearly $20 trillion in assets, enough to own every share in every company listed on the

London Stock Exchange at least three times over. In the average S&P 500 company (which counts global giants from Exxon and Pfizer to Amazon among its ranks), these two firms, together with State Street, control on average 20 percent of all shares, and continue to amass more. Moreover, this level of control is not limited to the US; BlackRock and other large asset management firms are global, controlling assets in all geographies and in every asset class, from stocks and bonds to private equity, government debt, commodities, and real estate. The global market for increasingly popular exchange-traded funds (pooled investment vehicles where shares in the fund can be traded like stocks on exchanges, providing greater liquidity and accessibility than mutual funds) is wholly dominated by just three firms, with BlackRock, Vanguard, and State Street controlling 80 percent of the market.[39]

In this sense, today's giant asset managers are markedly different from the predominant shareholders of the past. Not only has ownership been substantially reconcentrated, but rather than holding stakes in a handful of companies, large asset managers' portfolios are *universal* in the scope of their holdings. As a consequence, major asset managers' structural interest in the performance of any given investment is negligible. In contrast to the 'activist shareholder' concerned with individual performance of their small suite of investments, asset managers' *raison d'être* is accumulating ever more assets under management, from which their fees are derived.[40] Consequently, they are chiefly concerned with cornering market share in terms of new inflows of cash, and with consistently rising asset prices across the economy as a whole. Thus, to borrow from economist Mariana Mazzucato: 'much of fund management is a massive exercise in rent-seeking'.[41]

Compounding this structural disinterest in the actions of particular companies or even industries is the fact that the largest asset management firms have been propelled to their positions through the explosive growth of 'passive investing'. In contrast to the image of shrewd managers 'seeking alpha' and selecting stocks to beat the market, passive investors use indices – pre-structured lists of companies according to different criteria like market capitalisation or region – to construct portfolios that simply track the performance of a given market. And they're remarkably good at it – so much so that passive investments now constitute more than half of all assets under management in the US,[42] and are swiftly catching up in the UK.[43] Because the composition of the portfolio is largely fixed by the index, the threat of a shareholder 'exiting' a company to pressure it for changes in behaviour all but disappears. The rise of this 'asset manager capitalist' system of ownership thus undermines the fundamental assumptions used by its advocates to justify the shareholder value doctrine – yet we continue to live by it, with highly destructive results.

Living in the Age of Asset Manager Capitalism

While controlling 20 percent of shares in the average US corporation, as the 'Big 3' asset managers do, may not seem particularly impressive, the combination of this degree of concentration with the universal nature of asset manager portfolios is profound, and without precedent, ushering in a new era defined by Benjamin Braun as 'asset manager capitalism'. Imagine a corporation as a country: it would seem laughably undemocratic for just three individuals among thousands to have a fifth of all voting power. Now imagine that a handful

of individuals control this degree of power in the most influential countries all over the world, allowing them huge levels
of power and influence. This is the corporate world in which
global asset management titans find themselves. While the
comparison to nation-states might seem somewhat simplistic,
these managers together control increasingly make-or-break
quantities of voting power in the decisions at the world's
largest companies – many wealthier than national economies –
with world-shaping impacts. Moreover, because asset managers
must vote at AGMs, while many smaller investors and individuals lack the resources or interest to do so, the actual power
controlled by the largest asset management titans is often
significantly higher than the nominal fraction implied by
their vote share. And, despite an uptick in eco- and socially
conscious branding, they have regularly wielded this power to
crush societally beneficial changes, from voting against commitments to end supply chain deforestation to endorsing
outrageous executive pay packets.

Crucially, while corporate stocks and bonds still dominate,
they are not the only asset class owned by globalised asset
managers'. Asset management firms are buying up entire
neighbourhoods as assets at exorbitant above-market rates,
and hold large sums of Global South governments' debts,
borrowed on steep terms. At the height of the pandemic, the
G20 negotiated a temporary suspension of the extortionate
debt repayments that risked decimating seventy-seven of the
poorest governments' abilities to respond to the pandemic
(and indeed, consistently and unjustly limited their ability
prior to the pandemic to address other challenges like poverty
reduction or climate adaptation). However, the suspension
applied only to the bilateral debts between these governments
and those of the G20. A significant bulk of this – nearly a

third of eligible debt – is held by private investors, and was therefore exempt from the relief agreement, meaning that the temporary savings poorer governments might have made from suspending payments to G20 governments may have simply been a direct subsidy to private investors.

Much like the global banks before them, asset managers have quietly charted a course to systemic power. Perhaps most troubling, BlackRock (among others) is increasingly involved in activities directly in or adjacent to the state apparatus, including allocating the Federal Reserve's corporate asset purchase programme in response to the pandemic's economic shocks (through which BlackRock purchased stakes in many of its own funds).[44] BlackRock alumni are cropping up in prominent political positions the world over, including several key roles in the Biden administration. Even the financial press are now raising their eyebrows at the extent of crossover, with Bloomberg naming BlackRock the 'fourth branch of government'.[45]

This concentration is also not limited to publicly traded companies; private equity houses, which focus on buying stakes in unlisted private companies through their signature 'leveraged buyout', have experienced years of explosive growth and are now sitting on record 'dry powder' – that is, uninvested cash – totalling nearly £2 trillion.[46] The state of wealth concentration among the asset-rich is now so advanced, and conditions of systemic slowdown in advanced economies so acute, that at the start of the pandemic, investors were at a loss for 'investable' opportunities, forcing them increasingly outside of traditional stock markets and towards 'unconventional' areas, not least real estate. In the wake of Covid-19, with countless distressed companies, this 'dry powder' has exploded, with private equity taking control of significant swathes of the economy and set to take more. Unifying ownership and control, the explosive growth of the sector presages a further concentration of economic power. However, contrary to the industry's claims of investing in a productive post-pandemic future, extensive research details the extractive practices favoured by many private equity firms, including loading companies with debt (thereby reducing tax burdens) and asset stripping (such as selling company assets only to lease them back, with the private equity firm rather than the company retaining the cash from the sale).[47] The corporate form risks being ransacked further through the historic shifts in ownership underway.

On David and Goliath: a Democratising Agenda for the Corporation

We do not, then, live in the world envisioned by the advocates of shareholder primacy, nor in the socialised corporation imagined by Marx or Keynes. Instead, what has come to pass is a deep and ongoing monopolisation of ownership and control rights in the economy, epitomised by the systemic power of the asset management giants, with corporations increasingly reduced to vehicles for extracting income for passive rentier investors. How then can we reimagine the corporation as a vehicle for democratic production, resuscitating the emancipatory potential many have identified in the corporate form?

There is no way that, on the current institutional foundations, we can build a world where production is organised democratically to meet society's fundamental needs. Today, property is privileged over the security and dignity of the vast majority, who are subjected to exploitation, coercive dispossession, and the frontline impacts of environmental breakdown. Labour is ruthlessly squeezed, while the unwaged work of social reproduction that enables economic activity to go on is neither recognised nor fairly rewarded. Consequently, the root-and-branch transformation of existing patterns of corporate ownership and control is an essential precondition for enduring, society-wide change: extending democratic governance and planning into all aspects of economic life; reclaiming finance as a vital public function, not private power; deeply reorganising work and its purpose; enabling a justly managed reduction in working time; and liberating the power of generative enterprise and collective entrepreneurship to focus on meeting social and environmental needs.

A liberal property regime will not bring this future to life. Liberalism casts a veil of neutrality over the workings of 'the market', but turns a blind eye to the often violent processes by which property rights were made. It also increasingly fails to disguise how our current economic arrangement and patterns of ownership generate exploitation and exclusion by design, prompting escalating political rejection from the left and the right. Defensive social democratic reform, meanwhile, shies away from confronting the patterns of concentrated corporate ownership and speculation-driven allocation of investment that are currently failing to deliver basic dignity and security for much of the global population. Many of us intuitively recognise that, although we may live in formally democratic countries, 'democracy' is at best partial if limited to occasional votes at the ballot box. Power in the economy and consequently over our societies remains disproportionately vested in the hands of shareholders and corporate executives. We remain in many ways disenfranchised.

The task ahead is to replace private authority over production with a truly democratic and social institution that organises investment to meet needs based on work undertaken under conditions of substantive freedom within and beyond the firm. That means ensuring the question of the purpose of production is subject to democratic negotiation. The corporation is not in any meaningful sense a 'private' institution; to the contrary, it's a thoroughly public space, and one of the few that we have been content to maintain as fundamentally undemocratic. Why submit to the prerogatives of the rentier shareholder, managerial elites, and asset management titans, when economic coordination rights within and beyond the corporation could just as easily be organised to serve the many?[48] Reimagining the corporate form is no small feat, but in fundamental terms, the democratic economy begins where the primacy of property ends.

Reclaiming the Common Wealth: First Principles

The rights enjoyed by owners of capital are not natural, they have been constructed over time through sustained political effort and cemented beneath layers of legal precedent and codes written to construct and protect wealth generating assets.[49] In contrast to the idea that societal development has travelled along some inevitable path towards the 'end of history', the rights of different classes and peoples have ebbed and flowed, reflecting historically specific distributions of bargaining power within societies. We need only look to European or Chinese models of corporate ownership to see the range of possibilities, even within the parameters of the present. The dominance of ownership rights today does not stem from some innate efficiency or justice but power actively constructed and defended. Given that this construction is currently failing to secure basic well-being for much of humanity while providing the engine for climate and environmental catastrophe, the task we must set ourselves is to mobilise social power to transform corporate property relations.

To bring generative enterprise to life, we should reimagine the corporation as an institution of the commons: a social entity with multiple constituencies, who share distinct but overlapping economic and political claims on the resources of the company and outputs that supersede that of private ownership.[50] Because corporations are not in any real sense 'private', the primacy of private property claims should be replaced by democratic stewardship of the underlying resources and value of the company, guaranteeing key stakeholders voice, income, and control rights. This requires rejecting the fictitious private/public binary cast over the economy, which obscures how production is really organised and enabled: through institutions, households, and markets that are legally constituted and sustained by the public, and which can therefore be remade. The transition from a world of socialised production yet dominated by private property to one founded on stewardship and democratic control depends on transforming five essential features that condition how enterprise operates: purpose, membership, governance, capital, and networks.[51]

Corporations are presently oriented towards narrow financial purposes, measured in earnings per share, dividend ratios and the like, and defined by the doctrine of maximising profits to be skimmed by (often absentee) rentier shareholders. Instead, they should be made genuinely purposeful, oriented towards using our collective ingenuity to provide the material conditions and environments we all need to thrive, secured by decent and rewarding work for all who want it. Against the monopolisation of corporate voting rights by vast financial intermediaries, voting membership should be designed according to principles of democratic participation, whether in a modified corporate share structure or through new vehicles of purposeful ownership. Rather than governance by a nexus of capital markets, institutional investors, and senior executives, power over generative enterprise should be exercised by all key stakeholders, most saliently labour and representatives of social and environmental needs that are currently excluded. Instead of treating finance as if it is inherently scarce and limited, the democratic alternative would insist that in our post-capital-scarcity world, investment should be decoupled from the imperative of maximum private return, and credit democratically directed to serving genuine societal needs.[52] Finally, rather than a siloed system, wherein goods are traded based solely on price regardless of their wider, true costs, we need a system which recognises that prices are socially constructed, not just market driven, and embeds the corporation in socially guided and constrained markets (and non-markets) that bolster, rather than erode, social and environmental imperatives.[53]

Common sense as these changes might sound, they would have profound implications. If the nineteenth century saw the emergence of political democracy and the twentieth the emergence of social democracy, it is time for a third great wave of democratisation: delivering economic enfranchisement by replacing the oligarchy of economic power based on corporate share ownership with collective wealth based on social and economic participation. This in turn will require deep structural reform, not least in the recoding of law, the socialising of markets, the democratisation of economic planning, and the reorientation of our financial system to serve the needs of all of us.

Wielding the Tools

Economic power is codified and co-created by law. The primacy of property is the product of legal regimes developed to serve asset holders and structure bargaining power in their favour. Indeed, the law is an active tool for the creation of capital and its upward redistribution. But the law can also be harnessed for other ends, helping to build a more inclusive future. As Katharina Pistor has argued, the critical resources of coordination in the modern economy – money and capital – are not scarce. But the law encodes their scarcity in ways that generate extraordinary inequalities. Consequently, 'it is not that law only helps the rich; it is that the rich owe their wealth to the social resource we call law'.[54] Instead, the law could be used to unpick forms of false scarcity and broaden access to resources and services. As an inherently social resource, the law should support the meeting of *social* needs, creating new forms of collective voice and entitlement within and beyond the corporation.

The law also, as Sanjukta Paul has argued, naturalises and privileges a very specific form of economic coordination: production organised hierarchically within the for-profit corporation with decision-making monopolised by capital. Other forms of economic coordination, from producer coop-eratives to labour organising and strategic price controls, are prohibited or marginalised. However, because they are allocated through the public institution of the law, these 'economic coordination rights can be *re*-allocated – in the direction of economic democracy and cooperation'.[55] We need to return to first principles, asking why and how law allocates these rights, whether they should be related to ownership at all or based on more democratic principles, and why the current focus of legal ordering is to create financial assets, protect asset holders, and maximise their returns.

The potential impact of a root-and-branch reformulation of corporate and financial laws in the US or the UK cannot be understated. Though corporations have been granted the extraordinary legal privilege to incorporate themselves in virtually any jurisdiction of their choosing – a right to free movement denied to real persons – the majority of global company law is built around the legal systems of England or the State of New York.[56] A change in one of these jurisdictions could thus create a domino effect, with democratising potential that transcends borders.

Second, public power generates the structure of markets. Many mainstream accounts operate under a debilitating illusion: that 'free markets' both exist and are somehow pre-political, with interference constantly breaching the 'natural' sphere of economic life. Markets, however, are always made. They are inescapably political constructions enabled by the state. Background regimes of property, contracts, anti-trust laws, and so forth generate the context within which 'market forces' operate, as do the resources and rights that market participants are endowed with; these inevitably shape how they operate and for whom.[57] Unchecked, markets erode the conditions for their own survival, requiring 'intervention' and steering to reproduce and sustain themselves. Markets also require money and credit to operate, which are similarly constituted by public authority. Thus, in contrast to the 'spontaneity' usually ascribed to markets, they are in fact planned and maintained by governments and social actors who set the parameters for both how they operate and whose interests they serve. At the global level, far from the anarchy of competition, the functioning of the 'market' is carefully structured by institutions with vast planning power: central banks, financial institutions, and corporations themselves.

By insisting on the political origins of markets, and hence their malleability, we can begin to design them in radically different ways: to distribute, rather than concentrate, power, acting in service of meeting needs, and never taken as natural or inevitable. An agenda for democratic production will necessarily start from the understanding that there is no essential 'market' but an infinite range of possible markets. Freed from the illusion of a pre-law, pre-social market, we can reorganise their operations, ensuring through the law, collective organisation, and social provision, that people are endowed with the rights and resources they need to be free within and beyond markets. Even as we reimagine markets, we should reject the prevailing consensus that markets are both optimal and inevitable arrangements of human interaction. Contrary to Adam Smith's economic man, in human history markets are a recent invention.[58] A more just and ecological economy therefore begins with an honest appraisal of their uses and limits, and the recognition that markets must be subordinated to the needs of society – not the reverse.

Third, while the corporation itself is an island of non-market planning, that planning power is vested purely among executives and financial market actors to the exclusion, almost invariably, of all other stakeholders. This in-built capacity for planning should be harnessed towards collective flourishing, both within and between firms,[59] whether that be by providing better, more fulfilling work and expanded leisure time; developing human-centred technologies; furnishing the necessities of life to all; decarbonising society; or restoring the health of the natural world. This is not a question of planning versus markets but of discovering creative institutional mechanisms that wield the different powers of planning and markets towards these vital goals.[60] One example would be information.[61] The dispersal of knowledge is a key benefit of markets, yet the for-profit corporation has an interest in privatising information; to plan we need to know, and that will require new ways of sharing knowledge within and beyond the firm. This is all the more vital given how planning, and therefore accurate information, will be central to successfully decarbonising at the pace and equity required in the decade ahead.

At the same time, in a political economy defined by firms heavily leveraging their operations to survive and grow, and centred around maintaining outrageously high asset prices, central banks have become key agents of power.[62] They have the capacity to engineer the liquidity that plumbs the financial system, a public power that stems from states' unique ability to fund their own indebtedness – a power so strikingly evident during Covid-19. Left with little room to cut interest rates, central banks the world over have turned, in extraordinary scale, to asset purchasing programmes in order to suppress corporate and government borrowing costs by buying up their debt. But rather than simply keeping asset prices on life support, this systemically vital public provision of liquidity could instead ease the survival constraints of not-for-profit and other democratic forms of enterprise for the long term, helping expand the social economy and limiting the disciplining power of finance.

Financial markets, likewise, discipline the corporation, guarding against the possibility that they might begin to organise production for goals beyond accumulation. The stock market is also how capital 'exits' production in liquid monetary form, rewarding the ownership class. But money and credit are not inherent evils. Indeed, as David Graeber's seminal *Debt: The First 5000 Years* showed, relations of debt and credit are ancient, enabling us to pool resources in order to do remarkable things under commitments of reciprocity. Accordingly, finance has a central role in the democratisation of production and of the corporate form. As the financial economist Robert Hockett argues, 'private management of public capital inevitably results in mis-allocation (under-investment), ineffective modulation (over-speculation), and secular stagnation (under-production and under-development)'.[63] Alternatively, a public utility – oriented credit and banking system – underpinned by a network of public banks and a wider step change in public investment, aided by credit guidance – could mean a pattern of capital allocation that, rather than inflating prices, generates productive investment. This could take a range of forms, but in designing a democratic financial system two essential points stand out.

The first is that although they create credit, private banks do not control the money supply – borrowers do, by making the demand for credit.[64] The seeds of a democratic system, in which credit is created in response to need, are thus already there; however, the financial return profile of speculative investment in combination with the structural power of banks relative to those who borrow and their influence over the cost of borrowing – favouring corporate giants – heavily tilt the playing field, creating our glut of speculative borrowing and corporate debt. But the field is ripe for levelling if we are bold enough to limit needless speculation and lower the barriers of access to finance for initiatives that support a thriving society and environment, with the power of financial leverage wielded, instead, for the collective good.

The second point to bear in mind is that even if, on the supply side, we move towards a democratically determined and accountable supply of finance, we must also change the nature of the demand side. Simply allowing more finance to flow into a system in which shareholders retain the first claim on every dollar that comes in, and remain able to redirect profits towards their pockets, means that more access to borrowing by no means implies more investment. Thus, a financial system that actually supports societally important needs and goals cannot exist without the fundamental transformation of capitalism's engine: the corporation.

Property's claims against the corporation are vestigial – increasingly unjustifiable relics secured by power, not justice or efficiency. Today, they operate as a fetter on the productive forces of society and the development of sustainable abundance. It is high time for the functionless shareholder to be dethroned, and for new forms of mutuality, democratic power, and social purpose to be infused into the corporation's form. In short: citizens of the world unite, you have nothing to lose but rentier ownership claims!

4

The Commodified Life

We're the largest owner of real estate in the private world. And that asset class has boomed.
— Steve Schwarzman, CEO of Blackstone[1]

When it came to the foundational needs that sustain us – from housing to care – the pandemic unfolded with a cruel sense of irony, mediated by differences in ownership. While homeowners and landlords saw their asset values soar through the pandemic, for countless others, housing security was acutely threatened at precisely the time they needed it most. As the incomes of the working class were diminished or lost altogether, 'tenure-ism' (policy decisions and outcomes based on housing tenure) produced very different experiences of the crisis. Among richer economies, this was arguably most pronounced in the UK, where the contrasting treatment of renters and homeowners was in keeping with a political economy that increasingly resembles a 'housing market with an economy attached'.[2] While local authorities were given only £180 million in total to support hard-pressed renters during lockdown, wealthy homeowners enjoyed a holiday from stamp duty (land purchase tax) that cost the

Exchequer £6.4 billion, alongside a mortgage holiday from the chancellor.[3] In May 2021, the same month that the temporary eviction ban for renters in England came to an end, with half a million tenants at risk of losing their homes, the Office for National Statistics found that house prices had risen by 10.2 percent in a single year, the largest increase in more than a decade.[4] But this was by no means unique to the UK: North America and Europe also recorded record rises in real estate valuations during the pandemic.

A windfall for homeowners and landlords, certainly. But these policy choices reflected more than just political opportunism or pandering to a cohort of home-owning voters. They reflect the deep and decades-long shift to an asset-centred economy, wherein economic outcomes are increasingly predicated not only through an individual's relationship to production but also through their (interlinked) relationship to asset wealth. As Lisa Adkins, Melinda Cooper, and Martijn Konings document, the growth of the 'asset economy' has not only driven rentierisation, but also reinforced the centrality of intergenerational transfers to life chances, and constructed electoral coalitions in which voters are encouraged to view their interests and identity through the prism of asset ownership over work and employment.[5]

These shifting policy priorities and coalitions have propelled the meteoric rise of the investment industry through years of quantitative easing and, during the pandemic, acute and unprecedented expansion of central bank balance sheets to keep the asset economy afloat. Once relatively confined to the realms of the stock markets and corporate bonds, the asset management industry and all forms of investment manager are now gobbling up homes, a totem of the asset economy. In the US, Wall Street has bought up hundreds of thousands of single-family homes, often negatively impacting renters,[6] and frequently outcompeting regular buyers for these properties by margins of 20 to 50 percent.[7] At the time of the 2008 financial crisis, Blackstone, the US's foremost private equity firm, owned no real estate assets;[8] in the years since, buoyed by the opportunity to scoop up homes at rock-bottom prices in the wake of the crash, real estate income has grown to constitute an incredible half of the firm's income.[9] BlackRock, through its major interests in private real estate companies, is now among the United States' largest landlords. In the UK, the firm has been scooping up property assets with steady (often government backstopped) income streams conveniently attached, from senior living developments to social housing blocks, as well as private business property. The adult residential social care sectors of both Canada and the UK have become heavily populated by private equity firms, which, in many cases, load these companies with debt to enrich themselves, and in some cases lead these firms to collapse, with vulnerable residents' futures left hanging in the balance.[10]

Indeed, no industry fundamental to human life and well-being has escaped the interest of investment managers and private equity firms. The ability to dominate ownership of those goods and services that every individual needs to survive is a source of immense injustice, concentrating wealth for those with control over these vital assets while excluding many from access to the security and resources they need. To a great degree, the pandemic held a mirror to the broader and decades-long transformation of the way the necessities of life – shelter, care, energy, food, water, communication – are organised. From mixed or public models of decommodified provision and ownership, extensive programmes of privatisation have increasingly enclosed, commodified, and marketised access to these foundational goods and services. In turn, this has created a world of endemic rent-seeking based on exclusive private control of the things we all need to survive. In the process, governments have built durable political coalitions whose interests are now deeply interwoven with the increasing valuation of the assets they own, even as these same dynamics worsen the economic divide between the propertied and the propertyless. Two intersecting elements of this transformation exploded with traumatic effect in the pandemic: first, the ongoing privatisation of social reproduction through waning public provision, the growth of for-profit alternatives, and a crisis in our systems of care; and second, the increasing centrality of real estate ownership as a fundamental source of security (for some) and division.[11] These shifts have made our societies acutely vulnerable to shocks as social problems have been privatised and interlocking inequalities cemented.

Through an examination of shelter, care, and the right to communicate – all central to how the pandemic has been experienced – this chapter explores how the restructuring force of ownership has become a central institutional and political lever for reordering how our economies provide for (or more often do not) life's fundamental needs. While this is not an exhaustive list of necessities, these three are both essential to dignity and participation in contemporary society as well as major cleavages during the pandemic, whether due to the paucity of their provision or profound injustices in their distribution, linked indelibly to their ownership structure. In response, drawing on socialist feminist traditions, we argue that to dismantle the inequalities this generates we must reimagine and re-socialise provision. That means breaking with the primacy of property and market-led distribution to instead meet universal needs through decommodified means.

Residential Capitalism

We begin with the most basic of necessities: shelter. A safe, secure, and comfortable home is foundational to one's health and ability to thrive, yet in the US and UK, the housing market is arguably where the inequalities endemic to asset-dominated economies are most pronounced, and their implications most severe. In the US, house prices in May of 2021 were nearly 25 percent higher than the previous May, after a year of real estate market activity that rivalled levels last seen in the pre-crash mania of 2006.[12] In the UK, house prices surged by 13.4 percent, the largest year-on-year rise in seventeen years.[13] This extraordinary surge was an acceleration rather than a break with the norm. The stock value of British real estate rose almost a hundredfold from $60 billion in 1971 to an eye watering $6 trillion over the course of only four decades.[14] Vast increases in aggregate housing wealth, of course, mask deep racial and class-based inequalities, the result of decades of racist housing policy (both explicit and implicit).[15] This decades-long surge in wealth was actively facilitated by successive governments who, in response to systemic economic slowdown, incenti-vised a consumption-led growth model reliant on rising asset prices. The result: a worsening housing crisis where social housing is increasingly scarce, private rented accommodation unaffordable, and home ownership more and more out of reach for younger generations and low-income households.

This existing crisis interacted with the unfolding pandemic to devastating effect, with housing insecurity and poor conditions found to have a significant relationship with negative health outcomes, from higher likelihood of infection and illness to increased mental illness. Consequently, in societies that privileged owners over renters, whether or not they owned their home profoundly shaped people's experience of the pandemic.

This was not by chance. The credit binge that has helped drive asset-price inflation (mortgage credit in the UK expanded from £280 million in April 2020 to its highest-ever rate of £11 billion by March 2021[16]) was in part fostered by a combination of ultra-low interest rates and the Bank of England's expanded quantitative easing programme. While homeowners enjoyed record rises in their wealth, the pandemic was a brutal economic shock for low earners, the young, and the self-employed, who disproportionately rent. Many fell through the cracks: around 700,000 renters in the UK were served with 'no-fault' eviction notices after the beginning of the pandemic[17] while millions more renters and insecure homeowners across the world face the threat of losing their home. Moreover, as homeowners reaped an unearned wealth bonanza, private rents in Britain rose at the fastest rate on record in 2021, jumping by 9.9% outside London and even more in the capital.[18] With private renters now spending on average a third of their household income on rent, the rental market is now arguably the greatest upward redistributive mechanism currently operating in Britain, transferring vast sums from working households to asset rich landlords.

The growing chasm between the fortunes of renters and homeowners is the signature of the asset economy. In the

world's wealthy economies, class position and life chances
are increasingly 'defined less by occupational positions and
more by relationships to assets, especially to housing as a
wealth generating asset'.[19] There is no denying that an individual's relationship to the means and relations of production
through work continues to be fundamental in class location,
and a site of both domination and exploitation, but inequality
between those who own housing wealth and those who do
not has been cemented as a central divide. This in turn has
created a politically complex and challenging landscape,
with asset ownership an increasingly central determinant of
political sentiments.

In wealthier economies, the asset economy has entangled
a growing proportion of people in its logic, offering a flawed
bargain: don't complain about wage stagnation in exchange
for politically guaranteed asset-price inflation. From this
flows a new form of inequality that mixes the logics of
financialisation with the 'feudal' logics of inheritance to
reshape the social class structure as a whole.[20] Increasingly,
the ability to get on the housing ladder hinges on whether
an individual can access the 'Bank of Mom and Dad'.
Meanwhile, the centrality of assets introduces new tempo-
ralities and rhythms to capitalism based on the embrace of
speculative logics and the focus on generating sufficient
cash flow to service household and corporate debts.[21] These
credit-fuelled models of consumption have driven not only
rising inequality but also financial instability. This is not to
say, however, that rapidly rising prices mean the imminent
or inevitable collapse of the upwardly spiralling housing
market. So long as liquidity and leverage are abundant, with
lenders willing to extend credit to households and central
banks willing to backstop the financial system, the ratchet

is likely to keep gearing higher, if bumpily, in the years ahead. Sustained by the political alliance of the 'deflationary bloc', residential capitalism has been hypercharged by Covid-19. Absent political intervention, it is here to stay.

Home ownership is thus a disequalising dynamo of both exclusion and security. At once a driver of inequality *and* a critical source of wealth and reassurance for many millions, home ownership in Anglo-American societies is both complicated and politically disorienting. For many, there now exists an in-built preference towards rising real estate values not only with respect to their own home, but also through rapidly rising exposure via pensions to institutional landlords and real estate investment trusts. The political question of how we grapple with the housing crisis in the aftermath of Covid-19 is therefore a vital but complex challenge. One strategy would be to accept that the depth and scale of real estate financialisation is now irreversible, that the range of politically mobilised beneficiaries is too large, and so embrace the asset economy, seeking to further expand and universalise home ownership. However, a focus on simply extending private ownership risks distracting from the more fundamental goal at hand: ensuring everyone has a secure, safe, beautiful home regardless of whether they own housing wealth.

The other route then – more attractive but more politically challenging – would attempt to radically increase social provision and non-market allocation of housing in an effort to rein in the economic and political significance of home ownership. In practice, given the material stake hundreds of millions have in the housing market, in the beginning at least, a dual approach will be required to navigate the complex and variegated politics of housing, and its generational, geographic and class cross-currents. Our twin challenge is to expand affordable home ownership for those who want it (albeit while seeking to stabilise prices) *and* guarantee security and affordability for renters. From challenging the credit-based drivers of asset-price inflation, to increasing public and cooperative housing available for social rent; from commoning land to community land trusts and public-common partnerships; from instituting rent control strategies and reclaiming privatised social housing stock, to reasserting democratic planning of space and built environment, there are a wide range of approaches that meet the needs of a coalition of renters and ordinary homeowners.

The political need is urgent. The centrality of home owner-ship shapes our economies and our politics. Architects of the project that enshrined the primacy of property knew this well. Margaret Thatcher's introduction of 'Right to Buy', arguably her most totemic single policy, was critical to trans-forming not only the UK's housing tenure, but its politics. Enabling council house tenants to buy their house at a substantial discount, the policy helped consolidate a new political coalition for the right, centred on defending the interests of asset owners, regardless of the widely unequal patterns of ownership within this coalition. This was not some haphazard sale of public housing wealth; it was a targeted and successful effort to realign the interests of a new cohort of homeowners with wealthy asset owners instead of ordinary wage-earners, and with market-dominated over public provision. To understand its legacy, we need only look around us at the explosive spatial and economic inequalities that scar the UK's towns and cities. Yet Thatcherism's polit-ical insight – that changes in property relations targeted at clear social constituencies can anchor new political coalitions – remains fundamental. Unwinding its legacy will require grasping the centrality of ownership while building a future where a secure home is not dependent on entanglement within the asset economy.

Clapping for Carers

All crises generate their own rituals; Covid-19 was no different. Every Thursday evening at 8 PM throughout the first UK-wide lockdown, people gathered on their doorsteps to 'clap for carers'. But despite the applause, little changed. Care work, the work of sustaining and reproducing life, is the foundation upon which all our societies operate. From unprotected social care workers to unanticipated childcare demands amid school closures, the pandemic underscored both our dependence on unpaid or low-paid care (4.5 million people in the UK became informal carers during the pandemic alone), as well as the continued undervaluation of this labour in our economies and societies. Moreover, the gendered and racialised divisions of labour within our societies – most carers are women, and many are migrants – exacerbate other inequities.[22] However, while the crisis in care is rooted in capitalism's broader devaluation of reproductive labour, this is not its only cause. The interlocking forces of fiscal austerity, marketisation, and financialisation have transformed how we organise and reward care work, enabled by the turn to private ownership and provision of this vital need.[23]

Adult social care is emblematic of the ways in which private ownership models have hollowed out systems of non-household based care. Austerity reduced the resilience of the sector long in advance of the pandemic, but this weakness was anchored in structural shifts in ownership and control that, in several economies, have turned adult social care into a site of financialisation and rent extraction. In the UK for instance, in 1979, local government and the NHS provided two-thirds of residential and nursing home beds; by 2019, 84 percent of care home beds in England were in the private for-profit sector. This shift to a care sector dominated by for-profit providers has been in large part populated by private equity investors with a clear reason behind their appetite: consistent, publicly backed cash flows, real estate opportunities, and an ageing population make social care a compelling target for financial extraction.[24]

Profitable though they may be, there is strong evidence that for-profit care homes deliver worse-quality care than voluntary and public sector providers.[25] Care workers, meanwhile, face low wages and insecurity. In the UK, the average weekly pay for female care workers is just £385 a week, nearly £200 below the UK median. And the social costs of care work are borne not only by care workers and their families in a given country, but globally. As Fiona Williams, among others, has described, women in the Global South who migrate to become care workers are often forced to leave their own children or elderly parents behind, to be looked after by relatives or social networks, thus driving the formation of a 'global care chain'.[26]

Too often, our policy response has been to approach adult social care as a 'low productivity' sector in which productivity must be raised if wages and outcomes are to improve.[27] However, this approach – in addition to failing to grapple with the underlying devaluation of care work in society – suffers from an overly simplistic understanding of the relationship between productivity and wages, and neglects the distinctively human dimension of care.[28] It also fails to recognise, as the social theorist Isaac Stanley and others have argued, the significance of care as a collective service that secures well-being and dignity for care recipients and care workers, rather than simply a source of income and a series of 'bio-maintenance' tasks.[29]

Emblematic of this was the UK government's proposed solution to the crisis of adult social care, which it put forward in the summer of 2021. This 'solution' underscored the themes we have reiterated: despite calls for a wealth tax to support an increase in spending on adult social care (much of which would ultimately flow to private equity investors) the government opted to increase National Insurance contributions, a move that would hit wage-earners and the low-paid hardest. At the same time, there was no effort to transform the extractive ownership structures which have done so much to drive the challenges facing the social care system, nor to improve the quality of work for care workers themselves. Thus, the fault-lines of ownership cut through and severely limited efforts at reform.

Against the deliberate carelessness with which we currently treat both people and the planet, a truly caring world would nurture practices and institutions that recognise and value our essential interdependence and shared needs. As the Care Collective's *Care Manifesto* recently stated: 'We are all dependent on each other, and only by nurturing these interdependencies can we cultivate a world in which each and every one of us can not only live but thrive.'[30] From childcare to adult social care, from housework to our stewardship of the natural world, bringing this agenda to life requires undoing the gendered division of caring labour and centring care in all its dimensions. It requires recognising and then addressing how far our economies rely upon 'the off-loading of the cost of care onto the shoulders of underpaid and unpaid realms of society'.[31] Above all, we must recognise that care is not a private concern or responsibility, whether in the household or via for-profit providers, in either cases shouldered disproportionately by women, nor something to be managed according to the financial interests of absent corporate owners; rather it is a collective task. As Amia Srinivasan argues, 'the work of social reproduction must be the work of society.'[32]

Care, in all its forms, is neither a luxury nor a purely domestic concern, but a form of critical infrastructure and labour that requires transformative public investment and a reimagining of its distribution in society. Reversing the austerity programmes that have decimated care systems is a crucial first step. However, to secure an enduring shift to a new system of care, a transformation in ownership structures – essential as they are to shaping the organisation and imperatives of the care system – must be at the heart of this vision. Indeed, as researchers at the University of Manchester argued in the context of the heavily financialised UK care sector, simply putting more money into the existing system without removing the dominant interest of financial speculation and the drive to maximise returns will amount to little more than 'pouring water into a leaky bucket', siphoning this investment upward and outward to shareholders and private equity backers.[33]

We can begin by replacing the extractive and privatised nature of contemporary care provision with a public-oriented system: a coordinated system of cooperative, municipal, and publicly provided childcare and adult social care that centres life-making over profit-making.[34] Political economist of care

Emma Dowling, for example, argues for a new era of 'care municipalism' that can end the race to the bottom in terms of conditions, 'bringing social care (back) under the control of public bodies, where it can be planned and delivered directly, and democratising public ownership models in partnership with communities'.[35] Taken together, this would begin to socialise the essential work of social reproduction. An ambitious politics of care is also fundamental to the possibility of cohering a durable progressive majority. Care work is at the heart of the new working class: multi-racial, feminised, working predominantly in the service sector. And, as so evident during the crisis, care workers – paid and unpaid – are central to the functioning of our societies. They are a strategic pressure point for change, albeit currently fragmented. Cohering this latent political force through a transformative politics of care – democratic, decommodified, degendered – is an essential task for securing durable change.[36] By stressing the tension between the social nature of care and the privatised structures of property that push against our mutual interdependence, we can organise for a world founded on solidarity and mutuality.

Social-ist Networks

What we count as a necessity to meaningfully participate in society is never fixed. As the pandemic underscored, the right to communication, enabling the ability to work, learn, and play, increasingly hinges on access to high-quality, reliable internet. If, as the UN argues, we have a human right to communicate, today that means a human right to the internet. Despite this, for many, Covid-19 was marked by poor connection, expensive services, and uneven access to the means of communication. On the eve of the pandemic, only 2 percent of households in the northeast of England could access full fibre broadband, while in the US, 21.3 million people did not have access to the minimum speed broadband connection during the pandemic. And globally, of course, connection was very often far worse. A central reason for this slow and unequal deployment is the ownership structure of the entities tasked with delivering the digital infrastructures of the twenty-first century: the for-profit corporation.

Deployment of the full fibre network has exhibited classic signs of market failure typical when private corporations are tasked with building and maintaining nationwide infrastructures: shareholders reap gains; assets are sweated; investment is poorly coordinated and expensive, with costly and excessive duplication in some areas and severe under-provision in others; and the delivery of universal services requires large-scale public subsidy.[37] Relying on profit-making actors to deliver critical infrastructure has consequently left us with a heightened digital divide and reinforced regional inequalities, as these networks are characterised by high fixed costs and economies of scale that make its deployment unprofitable in rural or poorer areas.[38] The telecoms sector – a patchwork of publicly traded and private firms – exemplifies the rise of the rentier economy: income generated through ownership and control of scarce assets and infrastructure under conditions of limited competition – sources of wealth which often arose through the privatisation of nationalised companies and public assets.

By contrast, a twenty-first-century digital infrastructure can provide the conditions for a more democratic, sustainable, and prosperous society if it is democratically owned and decommodified.[39] We can readily de-privatise access to the internet and the infrastructures on which this connection is based;[40] doing so, however, will require moving beyond the 'regulatory state' and market-oriented approaches which have generated a rich stream of dividends for investors, but have entrenched inequality and slowed deployment for everyone else.[41] Moreover, market delivery is not only inequitable – it's inefficient. In 2018, an independent analysis commissioned by the UK government found that the fastest, cheapest way to deliver a 100 percent full fibre network was through monopoly provision, rather than market competition.[42] Indeed, the analysis suggested private providers would likely never achieve 100 percent coverage, as doing so was not sufficiently profitable without public subsidy.

Rather than leaving the development of vital digital infrastructures in the hands of powerful and opaque corporate actors, we should design them around the needs of ordinary people and communities. We should begin by making the rapid delivery of a 100 percent full fibre network, based on a publicly owned infrastructure company that can plan and deliver the investment and coordination necessary, central to our recovery plans. This model is not unprecedented: AB Stokab, a digital infrastructure company owned by the City of Stockholm, has delivered full fibre connections to 90 percent of all homes and 100 percent of businesses without using tax income, and dozens of companies now use the publicly owned infrastructure to deliver internet access. However, we can go further even than AB Stokab; if we are truly to decommodify access to the fundamentals of life, once the infrastructure is built, a publicly owned network can provide high-speed internet access free at the point of use to all households and businesses, with the maintenance costs covered through progressive general taxation. From there, other digital networks that provide vital necessities but which are currently being deployed slowly or used as sites for the consolidation of rentier power, such as cloud infrastructure, could be organised on similar principles. Taken together, democratic ownership, social planning, and public investment can underpin a decommodified digital future.

Twenty-First-Century Public Ownership

The case for providing the public infrastructures we all depend on through the tools of democratic planning and ownership rather than via the whims of private, profit-motivated actors and poorly coordinated market competition is not unique to full fibre broadband provision. Rather, the principle can and should be applied to the way we organise other fundamental near-monopoly sectors and services. Private, for-profit ownership of vital utilities is typically worse for workers, communities, and users, with asset sweating and the prioritisation of shareholders over investment. Across the world, this approach has been associated with a drive to reduce labour costs, hostility to unions, reductions in pension security, efforts to externalise social and environmental costs as much as possible, and the use of offshore tax havens and other tax avoidance mechanisms.[43]

Even on its own terms, the record of privatisation that the UK government pioneered (between 1980 and 1996 Britain accounted for 40 percent of the total value of all assets privatised across the OECD) is underwhelming. In his comprehensive analysis of the overall welfare impact of widespread privatisation under the Thatcher–Major governments, economist Massimo Florio found the shift to private ownership had little effect on long-term trends in prices and productivity; it did, however, contribute to regressive redistribution.[44] Privatising hitherto public wealth has a tendency to do that. Similarly comprehensive analysis of the scope and scale of public ownership in the US has also challenged misconceptions about its alleged inefficiency and underperformance.[45] Instead, the evidence suggests the privatisation agenda was centrally a project of class power, appropriating a private windfall for wealthy asset owners from public wealth built up through collective endeavour.[46] The result: the denationalisation and unwinding of national economies, endemic rent-seeking, and the prioritisation of shareholders' interests over the public – in other words, privileging a minority of private owners over the common good.

A return to social provision and public ownership – made democratic and accountable to its users and employees – can decommodify access to the basics we all need to live and thrive while putting power back in the hands of workers, residents, and communities. Indeed, the potential for public planning and coordinated investment opened up by a return to democratic public ownership makes building these institutions critical to the successful management of major social and energy-related transitions. From the collapse of Four Seasons care providers and the catastrophic failures of investor-owned utilities like Pacific Gas and Electric, to the endemic underperformance of the privatised railway, water, and energy companies, the failure of the status quo to deliver affordable, effective, and sustainable vital goods and services is as clear as its success in supplying infrastructure investor-owners with a reliable stream of risk-free income is obvious. As we face down the unprecedented coordination challenge of transforming our mobility and energy systems amid a deepening climate crisis, democratic public ownership of the infrastructures and assets involved would overcome a critical problem facing the transition. As J. W. Mason articulates: 'Treatment of our collective activity to transform the world as if it belonged exclusively to whoever holds the relevant property rights, is a fundamental obstacle to redirecting that activity in a rational way.'[47]

Importantly, reanimating public ownership, must not replicate the managerial, top-down forms that dominated – and, for complex reasons, often floundered – in the past. Instead, it can actively involve users, workers, and other stakeholders in governance structures, with enhanced public participation, accountability, and transparency. Unlike the singular focus of the for-profit corporation, public ownership can prioritise goals beyond the imperatives of profit maximisation. From municipal ownership of decommodified and decarbonised transport systems, to public retail banking, to public ownership of national energy grids, a new era of pluralistic and democratic ownership forms can best secure the conditions we all need to thrive.

5

A Shared Inheritance

Put your finger on each thing and ask, 'How did this get here?'

— Bertolt Brecht

What makes technological change happen? How are technologies – the artefacts, systems, and infrastructures that intervene in and reshape the material world – developed? Contrary to popular imagination, it's not merely the labour of cloistered geniuses working away on new developments, but the accumulation of knowledge and effort that has been passed down over generations. This knowledge is a common and social inheritance, yet knowledge and its products are increasingly enclosed behind private intellectual property regimes: a unique set of rights and protections that applies to the creations of the human intellect. Originally intended to encourage innovation and risk-taking by protecting ownership of knowledge and creativity, the dominant approach to intellectual property has now, according to researchers Thomas Hanna, Miriam Brett, and Dana Brown, 'increasingly become a central driving force for the accumulation and protection of assets by a narrow set of multinational companies and elite interests'.[1] The expansive, exclusionary forces of modern intellectual property regimes impose conditions of false scarcity where cheap and abundant forms of production and exchange could emerge, often with devastating results. Injustices that emerge from dynamics of enclosure and extraction are compounded by the fact the public sector plays a central role in many technological breakthroughs – innovation that is then habitually privatised and monetised by corporate actors.[2]

Nowhere is this contradiction clearer, between collective knowledge and its liberatory potential against the constraints of private property regimes, of the tension between technologies nurtured to meet needs instead of being driven by the relative profitability of investment, than the development and use of medicines. Vaccine apartheid is only the latest, starkest manifestation. One of the most notorious of such cases occurred in the autumn of 2015, when Turing Pharmaceuticals acquired the US manufacturing licence for the lifesaving drug Daraprim. Under the leadership of its founder, Martin Shkreli, the company raised Daraprim's price overnight by more than 5,000 percent, from $13.50 to $750 per pill. The consequences, for a drug the World Health Organization states is a critical medicine for any health care system, were predictably devastating. At a fiery House Oversight Committee over price gouging in February 2016, the smirking CEO was reprimanded in plain terms by Representative Elijah Cummings, a senior Democrat: 'It's not funny, Mr. Shkreli. People are dying. And they're getting sicker and sicker.'[3]

Shkreli, quickly nicknamed the 'Pharma Bro', and soon to be jailed on unrelated charges of securities fraud, made for a cartoonishly villainous figure. However, Big Pharma prioritising profit over the needs of patients was hardly an aberration. The US opioid crisis, which has claimed nearly half a million lives in the US, is also a vast source of wealth for some of the richest families in America, providing billions of dollars of revenue from the sale of highly addictive substances to often impoverished Americans. Other drugs have similarly shot up in price, pumping money into the already bloated balance sheets of pharmaceutical companies. Between 2007 and 2018, the list prices of seven branded insulin drugs in the US increased by 262 percent;[4] this in a country where one in four diabetes patients experience cost-related insulin underuse.[5] During the same period, the three manufacturers that dominate the insulin market, Eli Lilly, Novo Nordisk, and Sanofi, collectively distributed a total of $122 billion to shareholders in the form of buybacks and cash dividends.[6] Their behaviour epitomised the reorientation of the corporation in order to prioritise private owners, a shift from the model of 'retain and invest' to 'downsize and distribute', where the priority and focus of the company is on distributing cash to financial interests, particularly shareholders.[7]

Defenders of the status quo argue that profit is both an incentive for companies to invest and a source of cash to fund future innovative research. This is a generous interpretation of the sector's business model, to say the least. Due in large part to the patent system that grants monopoly over production, pharmaceutical profits between 2006 and 2015 outpaced profit in nearly all other industries in the US. Over the same period, the sector routinely spent more on advertising than research and development.[8] Even if a small proportion of the sector's profits are reinvested to develop new drugs, as political economist Rosie Collington puts it: 'Fundamentally, if a funding model to develop new medical technologies requires higher list prices that reduce patients' access to existing treatments, we have to question to what extent it is worth pursuing or even constitutes "innovation" at all.'[9] Instead, what these episodes suggest is that the obscenity of vaccine apartheid did not emerge *sui generis*, it grew instead out of a fundamental dynamic not unique to Big Pharma, but constitutive of contemporary capitalism: the enclosure of public knowledge through property claims for the extraction of private profit.

The effects of Big Pharma's enclosure of knowledge, so devastatingly evident during the pandemic, were recently summarised by Mike Davis:

> Big Pharma, the monopoly of monopolies, epitomizes the contradiction between capitalism and world health. Extortionate prices and proprietary patents for medicines often first developed by university and other public researchers are only part of the problem. Big Pharma has also abdicated the development of the life-or-death antibiotics and antivirals that we so urgently need. It is more profitable for them to produce palliatives for male impotence than to bring on line a new generation of antibiotics to fight the wave of resistant bacterial strains that is killing hundreds of thousands of patients in hospitals across the world. Big Pharma claims protection from antitrust laws because it is the major engine of drug research, when, in fact, it spends more on advertising than R&D. The cutting-edge pharmaceuticals and vaccines that it markets are usually developed first in small, dynamic biotech companies, which in turn capitalize research from public universities. Big Pharma, in essence, is rentier capitalism,

a fetter on the emerging revolution in biological design and vaccine production.[10]

Bursting through the fetters imposed by existing property relations will require transforming ownership so that technological development is organised to serve our shared needs. It is time to reclaim our common inheritance.

Burn Out

A short distance from the Brooklyn courthouse where Shkreli was convicted is Amazon's only warehouse in New York City, JFK8. The size of fifteen American football fields, it is the site for the technological consolidation of a modern caste system. In 2019, more than 60 percent of associates were Black or Latinx, while over 70 percent of management were white or Asian. This is scarcely unique to JFK8; the majority of the company's warehouse associates in the US are people of colour.[11] Subject to technologies that track every minute of their shift, and under the constant threat of automated dismissal if their productivity slackens,[12] workers are commanded, monitored, and disciplined by mass-management technical systems.

The result: work has intensified, and workers have been rendered disposable. Injury rates are double the industry average.[13] Indeed, despite working for a company that is one of the largest private sector investors in the world, Amazon warehouse workers have a higher injury rate than coal miners in the US. Even before Covid-19, Amazon lost an extraordinary 3 percent of hourly associates each week, a turnover of the workforce of 150 percent a year. In 2020, this staggering rate, twice that of the retail and logistics sector as a whole, accelerated. As online shopping surged, warehouse shipping records were smashed and three years' worth of profits were rolled into one; in the process, as a *New York Times* investigation into JFK8 found, 'Amazon's system burned through workers'.[14] To what end is this brutal and brutally effective system oriented? In whose interest is this oppressive panopticon of digital Taylorism operating, extracting enormous value from labour while treating it as expendable? Ultimately, Amazon is a machine for the enlargement of the wealth and power of its major shareholders. It is extraordinarily successful at that goal. During the first year of the pandemic, Jeff Bezos, founder and executive chairman of Amazon, saw his wealth nearly double from $110 billion to close to $200 billion. Returning from his maiden space flight in July 2021, he bluntly, albeit unwittingly, described the extractive processes that made this extra-terrestrial excess possible: 'I want to thank every Amazon employee and every Amazon customer because you guys paid for all this.'

The twenty-four-hour hum of Amazon's warehouses exemplifies the uneven and unequal ways in which technology has shaped the present crisis. New digital tools work alongside older forms of technology and labour discipline, with the experience of consumer ease enabled by the sweating of insecure workers. Inside the warehouses we see the ubiquity of surveillance technology across value chains, the intense imbrication of race and capitalism, articulated through unequal working conditions and health outcomes, and the entangled web of disciplinary tools that bear the imprint of class power. This entanglement has helped sustain the relentless rise of 'superstar firms' and the monopoly power of the digital platforms that control both frontier technology *and* precarious labour. Their extraordinary scale and logistical feats attest to the power and efficacy of non-market planning within the corporate form, even as they are organised in ways that amplify unjust hierarchies; a 'socialist Amazon' might share some of the same technical apparatus but would be fundamentally different in operation and purpose, investing in technologies that deliver radically divergent outcomes for its workers and users. Above all, the phenomenon of Amazon exemplifies the innate tension of capitalism: a social and economic system built on injurious class distinction where the working majority labour to enrich a wealthy ownership class, its generation of poverty amid plenty, technological development in service not of shared emancipation but private accumulation, with risk and reward structured through property relations that manifest in intensely racialised, unequal outcomes. Our common inheritance is leveraged towards the consolidation of vast private wealth.

The New Commanding Heights

Digital platforms such as Amazon now occupy the commanding heights of the contemporary economy. There is nothing new, of course, about the platform business model. From Renaissance banking houses and early modern stock exchanges, to the strip malls of the post-war years, our economies have long hosted companies whose business is intermediation and the siphoning of rent from suppliers or users of their space.[15] What's new though is the scope and scale of intermediation, now facilitated by digital technologies. Acting as gatekeepers for everything from social networks and rental apartments, to consumer commodities and taxi rides, platforms dominate an increasing range of sectors, generating revenue from subscription fees, commissions, and the monetisation of the 'attention' of platform users. Rapidly scalable, they trend strongly towards both standardisation and monopoly due to a combination of powerful network effects, winner-take-all markets, anti-competitive actions, and economies of scale.[16] Sitting at the heart of the transactions and engagements of the digital, and increasingly, the physical economy, they are rentier giants of our age, warding off or buying out potential competitors and batting away public policies aimed at curtailing their power. Taken together the reason for staggering market concentration is clear: 'monopolization is a feature, not a bug'.[17]

The pandemic is driving the ongoing consolidation of Big Tech's position as a central organising force of our societies. This centrality has made them unprecedented engines for the generation of revenue and shareholder wealth. Alphabet's net profit, for example, jumped by 162 percent to a record $17.9 billion in the three months to March 2021 as advertising revenue grew by a third. Indeed, the S&P 500's record year was fuelled by the five 'FAAMG' companies – the behemoths of Alphabet, Amazon, Apple, Facebook, and Microsoft – five companies that alone now represent a full quarter of the value of the index. Strikingly, since the end of 2017, with the S&P 500 up 23 percent, FAAMG accounts for about 72 percent of that performance.[18] More broadly, just fifteen companies in the index account for approximately 96 percent of the gain, meaning strong index performance increasingly conceals important information about which sectors are surging and which are stagnating.[19] What is masked by the spectacular gains of the digital giants, though, is a struggling corporate sector and increasingly cannibalised social realm. Indeed, as political economist William Davies argues,

> the appreciating asset value of the platform occurs through deteriorating social prospects elsewhere: what Facebook does for journalism, Spotify does for musicians and Uber Eats for independent restaurants. In each case, the basic means of access to a market or a public is privatized, and becomes an opportunity for rent extraction. This represents a new phase of what David Harvey terms accumulation by dispossession, only it is the infrastructure of civil society that is being seized, and it is rapidly capitalized start-ups doing the dispossessing, without the direct intervention of the state.[20]

In light of this, it is unsurprising that the dominant platforms are linked to negative social, economic, and political outcomes, both independently and in conjunction with their collection and use of data. From ubiquitous surveillance and the concentration of economic power, to the rise of algorithmic management (and bias) that hardwires discriminatory outcomes into core features of our economic system, our economic and social challenges are inseparable from the design and operation of the dominant digital platforms.[21] Whether the coordinating power of digital platforms can be transformed from the vanguard of corporate power into infrastructures of socially useful calculation is therefore an epoch-defining question.

Dreams of Datafication

In early June 2021 GP practices in England were given an urgent instruction. They were told to hand over their patients' entire medical histories to NHS England with just six weeks' notice.[22] Unparalleled in its scope, this vast data grab was justified on the grounds that pooling information would help improve care and develop new medicines. Yet the lack of transparency raised concerns: was the public's health data being forcibly turned over to be exploited for corporate profits?

Medical data is only one frontier among many in ongoing processes of 'datafication'. The platforms are transforming society into one vast digital factory. The impulse to collect, analyse, and monetise data drives an ever-expanding dragnet of digital surveillance and corporate accumulation of data. As a result, as Shoshana Zuboff argues, the largest platforms possess 'configurations of knowledge about individuals, groups and society that are unprecedented in human history . . . The problem is that all this knowledge is about us, but it is not for us.'[23] Rather than helping us to create planning and automating systems that can abolish unnecessary toil, this knowledge is used to fine-tune the manipulation of our behaviours, psychologies, and desires to create predictable human subjects – all to better generate income for the dominant platforms.

Yet data, despite being enclosed behind the walled garden of the platforms, is relational, and its value is in its aggregation. As the legal theorist Salomé Viljoen argues, its inherent relationality means we should view 'data not as an expression of an inner self subject to private ordering and the individual will, but as a collective resource subject to democratic ordering'.[24] Moreover, as a collectively created resource that becomes valuable in the aggregate, it defies typical classification as an asset class; indeed, what is striking is how far we are from the vision of some technologists of data being a tradable asset class in its own right. Private, properterian logics, whether individualised or corporate dominated, are unhelpful guides for data governance.[25] Nor is data dematerialised; the infrastructures that generate data are resource intensive, dependent on immense energy use and the consumption of resources derived largely from extractive industries. In this context, if we want a more egalitarian production and use of digital knowledge we must both re-politicise data and reclaim data infrastructures and their supply chains for the commons.

The Post-Human Mirage

Data is valuable in part because it is the 'raw material' for training machines to perform tasks that augment, or in some cases entirely replace, the need for human labour. As the pandemic ground a foundational institution of capitalism to a halt – the commodified labour market – there was frenzied discussion about whether it would hasten the deployment of data-driven automating technologies.[26] Rhetoric of the 'rise of the robots' loomed large once again as both promise and threat. Perhaps, the evangelists of automation claimed, humans' economic redundancy was at last, after many false prophecies, upon us.

Yet we are not on the cusp of a post-human economy. Despite striking advances in digital, physical, and biological technology, it is the absence of automating technologies – and the relatively slow pace of automation – that is more noticeable than their preponderance. Indeed, as Aaron Benanav has persuasively detailed, instead of surging productivity driving rapid technologically induced-unemployment, recent decades have been marked by a systemic slowdown in the global economy. The result: rather than job-destroying technological dynamism it is economic stagnation that is behind persistent under- and unemployment, rising inequality and insecurity, and stagnant wage growth. Rooted in global overcapacity and international competition which eroded profitability and then investment rates, it is this slowdown that has caused the slackening pace of job creation in economies that have been on the glidepath to slow growth. Attempted cures have failed to revive the patient. Indeed, they often misdiagnosed the cause and exacerbated the symptoms: chronic low demand for labour, sluggish investment, a weakening industrial growth motor, the expansion of insecure, low-productivity service sector employment, and the consequent fall in productivity growth.[27] In the Global North, this has manifested in stagnant wage growth and high levels of job insecurity for many with aggressive rentierisation and a proliferation of finance the central mechanism by which capital has sought to restore profitability. In the Global South, precarity and informal employment is the norm, with large parts of humanity economically triaged.[28] The result of all of this has been a rapid rise in inequality. As workers accepted wage stagnation and insecurity as the cost of employment, the gap between the average growth rate of real wages and of productivity levels widened, contributing, in Benanav's words, 'to the 9-percentage-point shift from labor to capital incomes in the G20 countries over the past fifty years'. If capital were broadly distributed, the transfer of income from labour to capital would have less severe distributional implications. However, that is clearly not the case. Indeed, 'worldwide, the labor share of income fell by 5 percentage points between 1980 and the mid 2000s, as a growing portion of income growth was captured by a tiny class of wealth holders'.[29] To take just one example of the uneven global division of wealth, Apple receives 60 percent of the market price of the iPhone 4, helping to enrich its shareholders, whereas Chinese assembly workers collectively receive 1.8 percent of the gross profits. In other words, the hallmark of our age – rooted in the malcoordination of global production as much as demand-sapping inequalities of distribution – is not the technologically-induced endpoint of work but economic stagnation and the consolidation of wealth and power that flows from rent-ierised, slowing economies. We may consider the glowing smartphone the sovereign marker of our technical age, but it is the army of platform workers – insecure, poorly paid, cast out from the legal protections of twentieth-century employment, sweating away to profit others – who are its true symbol.

Technology Is Political

Technology is intensely political.[30] It is about power: about who has the ability to intervene in the world, for which ends, and against whom. How it is developed and for what purposes is therefore a fundamental question of politics. Materials, infrastructures, economic power – all are profoundly shaped and reordered by the way technology is organised and deployed. From the knowledge systems that produced the vaccine to the tracking devices of the warehouse economy, technologies are social relations as much as technical artefacts. And it is not only its effects that are social. Technology emerges from a dense and shared inheritance of knowledge and investment. Too often this inheritance, and the plentitude it generates, is narrowly appropriated via private property.

Technology is not neutral – neither in how it is developed, nor in whose interests it serves. Its purpose and distribution are determined by those who own and manage it. Nor is technology autonomous. The pace and direction of technical change is shaped by the institutional arrangements that it is embedded in: who controls the allocation and rate of investment, and towards what goals, and the dynamism and priorities of the wider economy. As a result, technology is ambiguous – not inherently good or evil, but rather containing possibilities of liberation and oppression depending on how it is organised and governed, none of which is fixed. We will not be 'saved' by technology. Salvation lies with ourselves and our collective ability to remake our relationship with the world and the technical systems that shape it.

All of which gives us great latitude for change. However, to realise technology's emancipatory potential requires freeing its development from the command of capital and organising investment to improve work and address the climate crisis. As the Endnotes collective noted,

In a world given its predominant social forms by the imperatives of capital, it is of course to capital that we might look for explanation of the material imprints and patterns left by those forms – not just in the material-technological dimension of the production process itself, but also in all the material implications of this process as it unfolds across the surface of the globe.[31]

In this context, technologies are too often developed and deployed to extend capital's control over labour, heighten the unequal extraction of value, and surveil particular communities of people, rather than being used to meet human needs.[32] The consolidation of power and the generation of profit is the goal, not the elimination of drudgery. Nor has the trend been confined to the direct exploitation of labour power. From militarised equipment that has been used to police the Black Lives Matter protests to biased algorithmic management, existing technologies are 'bound up in the control, coercion, capture, and exile of entire categories of people'.[33]

Three problems arise when technological development is primarily yoked to the imperative of profit and the interests of wealthy asset owners. First, there is under-investment in the technologies and infrastructures we need but which do not generate profit (or, relatively less profit than other investments), whether that is labour-saving devices in the home, affordable life-saving drugs for curable diseases like tuberculosis,[34] or the rapid scaling of decarbonised infrastructures and industries.[35] At the same time, there is disproportionate investment in coercive systems of technological discipline that operate to extract ever-greater effort and value from labour. Second, investment is shaped by expected profitability rather than an assessment of needs which has resulted in under-investment and the slow deployment of new technologies, with many businesses preferring to 'sweat' labour over investing in much-needed technological improvements. Finally, the capital bias inscribed into our economies through the primacy of property means that the gains of technological change, where they do accrue, disproportionately benefit asset owners. Underlying inequalities of ownership therefore translate into the consolidation of wealth, income, and power. Absent political intervention, those who own the 'robots' come to own the world.

Towards a Technological Commons

What is at stake then is not technology itself, but the future technological development has in store for us if determined by capital's imperatives. Not platforms per se, but the immense power of Big Tech. Not the abolition of work through automating prowess, but the failure to abolish unnecessary forms of drudgery and toil because investment and production are organised for profit, not the expansion of freedom. Our challenge is to liberate technology and therefore ourselves by democratising the underlying architecture of ownership and control, consciously and collectively shaping their development and use. The task is to interrogate the technical systems that govern our lives, asking how they are organised, in whose interests, and whether they can be rearticulated away from the rapacious demands of profit-making and towards the deepening of human freedom and a thriving planet. Capital calls forth abundance and the potential of unalienated, emancipated individuals, but capitalist property relations fetter its realisation. As Martín Arboleda writes, 'science and technology will realise the plentitude of their soothing and creative powers once they break the spell that private property has cast upon them'.[36] The need is urgent. We are faced with a profound technological paradox: never has our collective capability – and need – to reimagine the world been larger, yet neither has the gap between potential and action. Why have we failed to deliver the unbelievable imagined inventions that captured minds in the early and mid-twentieth century? Why do nearly 1.5 million people still die of tuberculosis every year, when effective treatment has been available for decades? Why do technologies seek to intensify work rather than begin to build a world beyond toil? The answer lies in the extent to which we have enabled private dominion over advances that are ultimately the product of a long history of collective human endeavour.

Against property-based enclosure, then, we need to nurture a technological commons: a shared resource, stewarded for social benefit and individual flourishing, ensuring everyone has access to the services and resources to thrive, and with investment based on meeting universal needs. There are five areas where this can begin in earnest: ending data enclosure; reclaiming the platform infrastructure from Big Tech; democratising knowledge production and access; commoning calculating techniques; and instituting pro-labour automation strategies. We end here by exploring the direction we must move in each of these areas; in the conclusion, we set out the policies required to institutionalise this transformation.

Ending Enclosure

If 'surveillance capitalism' is totalising in its ambition, the progressive alternative must be similarly systemic in response. We need a politics of data that is concerned not just with the distribution of data, but its production as well. About why and how data is collected in the first place, based on what forms of governance. We must challenge data extraction, prohibiting it where necessary, not just rethink the terms of access and use after its collection. Ubiquitous surveillance, hardwired into the for-profit corporate platform and the capitalist state alike, must be broken if we are to unpick the ways data currently entrenches inequality, power disparities, and social oppression. As Salomé Viljoen argues, an egalitarian technological future means moving from an individualised response centred on notions of private property towards questions of democratising data governance as a whole.[37] At the same time, the potential for data is limited when the ability to analyse datasets – turning aggregated data into actionable information – is narrowly held, with analysis typically undertaken in the service of profit maximisation or the enforcement of dominating state power. Liberating the general intellect, the combination of technological expertise and social knowledge that our era of computational power and granular data contains the seeds of, requires expanding who has the ability to analyse data towards different ends.

Building a data commons in place of enclosure is fundamental to bringing this vision to life. This would collectively define the rules by which data can be collected, justly manage access and use, and broaden who can analyse datasets under appropriate conditions.[38] In doing so, it would help us think more sceptically about the type of 'dataworlds' we construct and for what purposes they should be organised.[39] Above all, a commons would steward data as a collective resource whose value is inherently social, a resource governed democratically, not owned and controlled privately. As Viljoen argues, this means data should not be treated as an individualised, tradable commodity – whether held by a person or corporation – but as a social relation encoded with particular qualities; overcoming 'the inegalitarian harms of datafication will require democratising these social relations'.[40]

A Common Platform

Resculpting our dataworlds will require that we reshape a key intermediary of data collection and analysis: the platform. The infrastructure of the platform, a digital space to connect, coordinate, and communicate, contains extraordinary potential. Indispensable to how we live, work, and play, their collaborative and networked nature makes them ideally suited to multi-stakeholder models of governance and ownership, giving suppliers and users genuine voice and control. Currently, though, they are engines of inequality and surveillance. Liberating the platform's democratic, enlivening potential will require that we challenge the behaviours and outcomes that are generated by the governing logics of corporate ownership and profit maximisation.[41]

A first step will be limiting the power of platform monopolies through progressive anti-trust action; the appointment of Lina Khan as chair of the Federal Trade Commission augurs well for efforts to constrain their power. The goal must be to turn them into utilities based on global multi-stakeholder governance, democratic ownership forms, and anti-surveillance principles that end the digital panopticon. Platforms that act as labour intermediaries, like ride sharing apps, can be reorganised as digital cooperatives that give suppliers and users voice and rights. Scaling an ecology of co-owned or democratically managed platforms that provide socially useful functions will require a range of interventions, incorporating both bottom-up and top-down strategies for change, sensitive to the needs of place and political context. Ambition and experimentation will be key. Law, as both an active shaper of how the platforms operate and a facilitator of their monopoly power, can help reorganise them and dismantle existing forms of digital rentierism. One thing is clear: if we reject disempowering notions of technological inevitability, we have the tools to 'recode' the platform and revive democratic control of our digital infrastructures.

Democratising Knowledge

The current intellectual property regime is associated with a series of negative outcomes: increasing inequality, growing corporate power, monopolistic reductions in competition, and slowing rates of innovation in many fields, among others.[42] The Covid-19 vaccine embodies this. Here was an extraordinary collaborative achievement of public and private effort, made possible by dense layers of investment, infrastructure, and shared knowledge. Yet its production, distribution, and use was organised along principles of property not need, to generate profit instead of guaranteeing affordable medicines and medical supplies. While countries in the Global North bought vast quantities of vaccines, often far more than they needed, those whose governments could not afford or who were denied access to the IP have been left without. To secure conditions of shared abundance we must necessarily challenge this exclusionary logic, defending and expanding the knowledge commons against expropriation and predation.

This will require social struggle to build a new set of institutional foundations that recognise that knowledge is a collective creation, whose production and organisation should reflect that. A transformative and sustained increase in the size of public R&D investment can anchor this, focused on addressing our intersecting economic, health, social, and ecological crises. New commons-based, collectively owned regimes of basic research that reject the time horizons and profit-oriented characteristics of financialised research can deliver much needed technological breakthroughs and techniques for their dispersal. The commoning of knowledge generated through public investment can ensure collective advances deliver social benefits, not just private wealth. Finally, a knowledge commons must be solidaristic in operation. The wealth, knowledge, and resources of the Global North depend on long histories of unequal resource extraction, enslavement, and imperialism. To begin redressing this, we must build a reparative global technological commons. This agenda is urgent: the pandemic has underscored just how deep the devastation caused by the encasement of knowledge in the folds of corporate power runs.

The Calculation Debate

But it is not just knowledge that is being enclosed. Techniques of measurement and calculation are equally vital instruments of governmentality and power. The political question is: Calculation for whom? Today, powerful infrastructures, from algorithmic management to the ubiquitous ratings and 'nudges' of our digital selves, are geared towards organising the complexity of social life for the narrow pursuit of profit maximisation. Extraordinary potential is funnelled into unequal and limited ends. Instead of strengthening forms of cooperation and mutual planning for societal benefit, calculation is driven by the prerogatives of property.

Against this, we need to common the tools of calculation and coordination. Planning is ubiquitous, it must now be made democratic and social in both practice and orientation. This is about ensuring the design of the algorithms, feedback infrastructures, and protocols that process, organise, and act upon data can be adapted, shaped, and co-designed by those impacted by them.[43] It is about making relevant forms of information accessible and actionable. As the economist Otto Neurath noted in 1925, if democratic socialism is to grow, society 'must know from which conditions it starts at a certain moment and what it can undertake . . . above all the labour movement needs a statistics of the conditions of life'. Calculation requires a data commons to better understand those conditions. And it is also about embedding institutions of everyday democracy in the workplace and communities to redistribute decision-making, from strong collective bargaining and information rights for workers to empowering people at a neighbourhood level to shape their built environment. In doing so, we can organise social and economic life through democratic control, not private power. That, though, will require a break with the primacy of property in the organisation and hierarchical interests of economic and social planning. If we can develop a thicker democracy, renovating and expanding past the institutions of representative democracy, then the technologies of calculation and planning can be retooled for the common good.

Automation for the People

Automation has the potential 'to free up purposeful human activity, to free millions of the necessity of work. But there is no inevitability to this process, it must be struggled for and won.'[44] That requires a strategy for democratising automation that acts on four insights: technological development and use is currently designed to institutionalise capitalist power, not maximise societal welfare or individual flourishing; rates of technology adoption and innovation will remain suboptimal so long as investment decisions are guided overwhelmingly by the profit imperative; investment is about power and the relations it sustains or transforms; and, absent the democratisation of our economies, the gains of automation are likely to compound existing inequalities. To manage the acceleration of automation justly, we need a threefold approach addressing these interlinked challenges.

First, we need to pursue public-led industrial strategies and increased public investment to maintain full employment, lighter work economies, where everyone who wants a job can have one but where we work less on average, if we are to drive the uptake of automating technologies on pro-labour terms. This must extend beyond 'frontier' firms towards sectors that represent the 'everyday economy' and into the household economy. Second, to ensure the evolution of technical systems is geared towards emancipating our time and capability, not extending unaccountable forms of power, we need new channels for shaping technological development. Whether that is through a direction-setting role for public investment, or by empowering labour to design how technologies are adopted and used, technologies must be developed to complement human creativity and autonomy. We need a 'Lucas Plan' for every workplace, with the tacit knowledge, skills, and needs of people driving the democratic reorganisation of production. Third, maintaining the volume and direction of investment needed to maintain a high-pressure economy will necessitate enacting Keynes's prescription for a 'somewhat comprehensive socialisation of investment.' This goal will undoubtedly meet organised resistance that must be matched by popular political struggle, but it is the only way to durably overcome the policy-induced economic stagnation – via austerity, rentier-isation, and under-investment – that have plagued our societies. This kind of an agenda will only be possible if we make the acceleration of automation on pro-labour, pro-social terms a political demand. Absent these institutional arrangements, uneven processes of automation in a world of low growth risk deepening a paradox of plenty: the advance of technical systems will expand social wealth and collective capability, but this will be narrowly and privately appropriated through inequalities in ownership. If, though, we democratise ownership and control, then the advance of our collective capability can secure the conditions of material security and freedom for all. In the process, our expanding capacity can help us progressively reclaim our most precious resource of all from the command of capital: our finite time.[45]

Abundance Is a Social Relationship

Technology provides an aid, not an exit from the need for a transformative politics of production and distribution. Overcoming socially determined scarcity will ultimately depend on political organisation, not technical fixes. As the political economist of employment Aaron Benanav eloquently puts it, 'Abundance is not a technological threshold to be crossed. Instead, abundance is a social relationship, based on the principle that the means of one's existence will never be at stake in any of one's relationships.'[46]

Together we can guarantee collective abundance and material security for all. However, currently our common wealth is being appropriated by the few, while the processes of exploitation and exclusion deepen – of warehouse labourers, of our personal data, of those suffering illnesses without access to long-available cures. Genuine freedom that is not dependent on the exploitation and unfreedom of others will require us to reimagine not just how and to what ends technologies are developed and used. It will also, in an era of accelerating environmental breakdown, depend on our ability to reclaim technological innovation and transform it from an engine of unsustainable wealth extraction and concentration to a vehicle for collective emancipation. Emerging from our common inheritance of knowledge and infrastructure, our technical potential must be emancipated from capital's imperative. Democratising technology is fundamental to liberating technology – and liberating ourselves.

Robbing the Worker and the Soil

We thought it was oil, but it was blood.
— Nnimmo Bassey, Nigerian environmental activist

The Niger River Delta is home to Africa's largest mangrove forest, a remarkable ecosystem capable of storing twice as much carbon as a terrestrial forest. Between labyrinths of submerged roots, mangroves conceal a dizzying array of plant and animal life, breathing oxygen into waterways and sustaining vast wetlands rich in biodiversity while supporting the livelihoods of millions of local fishers and farmers in the Delta. It is also one of the most polluted places on Earth. Hemmed in by a maze of decades-old, often deteriorating pipelines owned by the likes of Shell, Texaco, and Exxon, the Delta has endured thousands of oil spills since extraction began in 1958. Some estimates suggest that as many as 40 million litres of crude oil pours into the area every year – with near impunity for the companies involved. Gas flares and toxic runoff choke the air and the water table. The result is devastation: thousands of kilometres of mangrove forest have been destroyed or are at risk, wiping out ecosystems and livelihoods, while adjacent farmland has been flooded with oil. Rates of cancer, neurodegenerative disease, and birth defects are all abnormally high.[1] A recent study estimated that in 2012 alone, 16,000 Nigerian infants died within their first month of life due to oil pollution in the Delta.[2]

In 1994, a military task force (allegedly with backing from oil giant Royal Dutch Shell) was established to put down a protest against Shell's operations in Ogoniland.[3] After the protest was crushed, nine local activists were executed for their involvement following a sham trial.[4] Military enforcement continues to cast a long shadow over the region, with residents subject to routine intimidation and violence.[5] Despite the wilful destruction and neglect of the Delta's delicate and vital ecosystem over several decades, and accusations of violence against its people, Shell has come away relatively unscathed, even carving out a place as an apparent 'leader' in the oil industry for its much-publicised U-turn to a 'cleaner' future. In February 2021, Shell announced it would become 'net zero' in its operations by 2050, affirming its commitment to 'generating shareholder value, achieving net-zero emissions, powering lives and respecting nature' – in that order.[6] As a cornerstone of this initiative, it began championing 'nature-based solutions' to the climate crisis, namely mass tree-planting projects to offset the firm's emissions. But beneath the glossy press coverage and leafy promotional videos lurked a darker reality.

The much-touted 'nature-based solutions' at the pledge's heart generally involve firms or individuals paying to 'balance out' their carbon emissions by restoring or preserving part of an existing carbon 'sink', like a forest. In practice, this can mean anything from simply not destroying an ecosystem that would otherwise have been razed, to replacing a felled woodland or planting a large stand of trees in a new location where there was no forest cover to begin with, a process known as afforestation. By definition, these solutions require carving off large parcels of land in order to 'balance out' emissions made elsewhere – in Shell's case, in its production of millions of barrels of oil per day. Crucially, as the charity ActionAid and others have highlighted, this often means expropriation of land from local communities, farmers, and ecosystems – largely in the Global South – to sustain the demand for emissions from corporations in the Global North.[7] In this context, Shell and its contemporaries' supposed 'pivot' to a lower carbon, more 'sustainable future' is nothing of the sort. Rather, it is a continuation of the expansionary logic that has driven the extractive economy for generations: the unceasing enclosure of new domains for profit. Now, pushing against the limits of its own expansion, the fossil fuel economy must enclose what remains of nature and available land to perpetuate its own existence.

In January 2021, after a years-long legal challenge, Shell was found liable for damages to farmers in the Niger Delta caused by pollution from its infrastructure. The company said it was 'disappointed' by the verdict. In May of the same year, Shell laid out its first 'green transition plan' to shareholders at its annual general meeting, where CEO Ben van Beurden said the firm's operations in the Niger Delta were no longer compatible with its ambitions, and they could not 'solve community problems' in the area.[8] When they go, they'll have claimed thousands of kilometres of a once-thriving ecosystem and many lives for their profit. In a twist of irony, at this same AGM, Shell announced net-zero targets that will require an area of land three times larger than the Netherlands so they can keep digging up fossil fuels for decades to come.

Green Capitalism and Fossil Fascism

Outright denialism regarding the climate and ecological emergency is in decline, increasingly relegated to the fringes of the reactionary right. As resource scholar Thea Riofrancos has written, the question that will come to shape global politics in the coming decades 'is not whether to decarbonise, but how'.[9] At the heart of this existential question is a struggle over who is entitled to the essential riches of the planet, from land to minerals, and who will be excluded. This battle is increasingly being dominated by advocates of 'green capitalism'. These are the politics of the European Green Deal, the British Conservative Party's so-called 'Green Industrial Revolution', and, with some exceptions, Democratic representatives in the United States. This apparently greener, kinder capitalism is also promulgated by powerful international institutions from the World Bank to the The United Nations Framework Convention on Climate Change. Within this programme, the current economic system both can and should be disturbed as little as possible in the transition to a decarbonised society. Its path is littered with cap and trade, carbon taxes, 'ESG' (environmental, social, governance) investing, and the crowding in of the supposedly more innovative and efficient private sector by using public fiscal and monetary power to 'de-risk' private capital, rather than investing directly. It is predicated on the virtually one-to-one replacement of our existing vehicle fleet with electric vehicles

(EV) rather than mass and multimodal transit; enormous renewables deployment to sustain growing domestic energy demand; and the rollout of frequently unproven technologies at a planetary scale.

Marching in steady opposition is the force of what Andreas Malm and the Zetkin Collective call 'fossil fascism', the unification of ultra-nationalist far-right politics and those of ecological absolutism, often manifest in chauvinist and anti-immigrant policy as the panacea for environmental decline.[10] In contrast to previous decades' denialism, there is frequently no outright denial of human-induced climate crisis in the context of fossil fascism, nor is the urgency of environmental protection ignored. Instead, it seeks to marry these imperatives to a nationalist and routinely violent thesis that identifies growing populations in the South, and their increased migration northward, as the cause and threat of environmental breakdown.[11] Nor is this thesis merely confined to the conspiratorial fringes. It is routinely visible in mainstream politics, from Bolsonaro's violence against Indigenous people in the Amazon, to France's National Rally proclaiming 'the best ally of ecology is the border',[12] to Nigel Farage – forever at the vanguard of British xeno-phobia – joining the board of a firm which invests in carbon offsetting schemes.

Ultimately, both these strains of politics aim to preserve, or indeed further entrench, particular distributions of wealth, access, comfort, and power – what scholars Ulrich Brand and Markus Wissen have termed an 'imperial mode of living'. In this view, any action taken on the climate and environmental crises must maintain the level of private affluence and security enjoyed by particular classes (largely but not exclusively located in the Global North) based on '(in principle) unlimited access to labour power, natural resources and sinks', in some 'elsewhere', whether that implies the extractive zones of the Global South or the exploited labour of agricultural and factory workers within wealthy countries themselves.[13] Thus, while green capitalism is often coated in the veneer of progressiveness, the agenda is nonetheless predicated on upholding existing systems of enclosure, concentration, and exclusion. It is simply quieter about its foundations in violence.

However, the inherent tendencies of the global capitalist system – enclosure, concentration, expansion – are increasingly undermining the very preconditions for its existence. Immense concentrations of ownership and control have produced inequalities in wealth, consumption, and power that cannot be sustained ethically, ecologically, or indeed politically. Concurrently, interminable expansion and extraction means we are rapidly running out of 'elsewheres' to be exploited, whether this means cheap labour, new sites for natural resource extraction, or sacrifice zones for housing or neutralising our ever-greater wastes.

The Niger Delta, its people, and its biodiversity have become a symbol of the violence and destruction of our fossil-fuelled economy. Corporations designated the Delta a sacrifice zone in the service of profits and the energy and resource demands of the global wealthy. It is a totemic, invisible 'elsewhere' of the sort demanded by both green capitalists and fossil fascists. While the delta is incredibly productive, providing some 40 percent of the United States' crude imports and 75 percent of the Nigerian government's revenue, very little of this is realised as investment in local communities and the environment.[14] Despite these natural riches, just 30 percent of its residents have access to clean drinking water, and, at just over forty years, life expectancy is a full decade lower than the national average.[15]

The past few years have seen a significant acceleration in the pace and volume of climate policies, pledges, and actions, mirrored in escalating public concern and demands for action. In the UK, a 2050 net-zero target was enshrined in law, while in the US, the Biden campaign championed a net-zero target for electricity generation by 2030. Oil majors have been held accountable in courts for the need to align their business plans with the Paris Agreement. But critically, of the programmes we've seen, none come close to grappling with fundamental questions about the economic and political inequalities and injustices that underlie ecological crisis. Thus, even our primary 'hopes' still have yet to break with the green capitalist framework – a reticence that will define the struggle over ecological crisis in the coming years across two frontiers: who 'owns' the resources needed for decarbonisation, and who 'owns' – via exclusive access to carbon and environmental sinks – the right to destroy.

In 2015, Oxfam published its now-seminal study on carbon inequality, finding the wealthiest 10 percent of the global population responsible for half of all lifestyle emissions. Since then, numerous estimates of the inequalities in emissions, energy, and resource use have added to the weight of evidence supporting the fundamental truth: that the world's wealthy – largely but not exclusively living in the Global North – consume far more than their fair share, not only of resources and productions, but increasingly of carbon 'sinks' to offset the pollution. Importantly, despite the reasonable assumption that this 10 percent comprises a class of private jet-setting elites, the wealthiest 10 percent of the world's population earns the equivalent of just

£27,000 per year ($35,000). If you live in the UK, this would place you below the median income of nearly £30,000 – hardly a lavish income when confronted with the cost of living. But crucially, these carbon inequalities hold *within* countries as well: according to Oxfam's analysis, the highest 10 percent of earners in the UK emit five times more than the bottom half, while 2.5 million households – some 10 percent – live in fuel poverty.

This is not to say that only billionaires need to curb their emissions to address the climate crisis (though this is both good and necessary), nor that – in line with the widely repeated and often-misused statistic that 100 companies are responsible for 71 percent of global emissions – changing how those of us in the Global North live is futile. Rather, it implies an honest reckoning with the hard truths of the global economy: maintaining the daily life of a middle-class worker in the US, while hardly extravagant, is nonetheless predicated on the exploitation of cheap labourers – in agriculture, extraction, and domestic and international manufacturing – as well as the degradation of natural resources and sinks in an often invisible 'elsewhere', whether in the poisoned water of Flint, Michigan or the Niger Delta. A single open-cast mine, with the majority of its product destined for consumption by the globally affluent, can produce up to forty times more solid waste in a given year than a Latin American megacity.[16] Resolving ecological crises is therefore a project of distribution and power, which requires overcoming the dynamics fundamental to capitalism – enclosure, concentration, and expansion. Anything less than this is doomed to fail.

What's Yours Is Mine: Resources of the 'Green' Transition

Little embodies the agenda of the green capitalist – nor its inherent unattainability and unsustainability – like the jubilation surrounding electric vehicles (EVs). Electric vehicles have become the touchstone of liberal climate policy, seen as a palatable 'win-win' policy in which individuals and manufacturers can be subsidised to change behaviour, drivers can save on energy costs in the long term, and crucially, no disruption is needed to the highly atomised, space- and resource-intensive mode of private transport that now defines Anglo-American capitalist societies. The Achilles heel of the race to electrify the global vehicle fleet is that EVs are not created in a vacuum. Their production requires considerable material throughput, and their carbon-saving capacity rests on their batteries, for which lithium is the essential resource. Lithium is also currently the primary means of energy storage for all renewable grids, where a similar rush to build is generating a huge surge in demand. In its 2021 report, the International Energy Agency predicted that to reach global net zero by 2050, we will need to produce six times more critical minerals – such as lithium, copper, cobalt, and rare earths – by 2040 than we do today. But for lithium, driven largely by an anticipated explosion in private EVs, this growth in demand is expected to reach more than fortyfold within twenty years.

To meet this growing demand, corporations, investors, and governments have been hungrily eyeing new opportunities for lithium extraction. Yet despite the existence of significant deposits in the United States, environmentalists and other local groups have successfully raised repeated objections to these new projects. There have been loud concerns raised about local ecosystem disturbances or, in the case of Nevada, over the disturbance to the habitat of a particular endangered flower. Well intentioned as these efforts may be, they stand in stark contrast to the lack of protections afforded to other communities living on the borders of extractive industry. While Australia has long been the world's largest producer of lithium, many are now turning to South America for their supplies, where between half and three-quarters of the world's unexploited lithium is thought to be located in the 'Lithium Triangle' that snakes along the borders of Chile, Bolivia, and Argentina, and where most known deposits are hidden in the austere and beautiful landscape of the Atacama salt flats.

Lithium extraction in the Triangle has come with ecological devastation, water table pollution and depletion, human rights abuses, and the displacement of Indigenous populations, who have been largely excluded from the industry's rewards. Of the five largest lithium producers in the world, only one had a human rights policy as of 2019.[17] The methods used by corporations mining in South America consume 500,000 gallons of water to produce a single metric tonne of lithium, depleting local reservoirs in drought-prone communities on the frontlines of the crises, and threatening the vulnerable ecosystems that thrive in the Triangle. Despite this, extraction and expansion in the region continues apace, and investors anticipate the Triangle will become the world's primary source.

As the global economy looks towards a newly booming resource sector amid post-pandemic 'green recovery' packages, this enclosure will only accelerate, stretching into new and increasingly precarious domains such as deep-sea mining. Already, deep-sea exploration licences have been granted for tens of thousands of square kilometres in the western Pacific, threatening delicate ecosystems and the communities dependent on them.[18] But who has the right to grant these licences? As an inherently global ecosystem defined by mass migration of species and planet-spanning currents, how can the ocean floor be granted to private authority in the pursuit of profit?

So while two mines in as many years have been blocked in Nevada over environmental concerns, multinational corporations continue to expand their operations 'elsewhere', where calls for justice are easier to ignore. This two-tiered system for valuing human life and the environment is not an aberration but a feature of a 'greener, kinder capitalism'. As geographer Martín Arboleda writes: 'The self-objectifying practice of capital has metamorphosed into rivers poisoned by mercury and cyanide . . . peasants ravaged by debt, police forces bizarrely out of control, mining towns riddled by cancer epidemics, and rampant labour casualization.'[19] Without a root-and-branch reorganisation of the way we steward and use the planet's resources, powerful corporations will continue to enclose, extract, and deplete them to support the 'green' demands of the global affluent, to the exclusion of the world's poor majority. And while Atacama's salt flats are a totemic example of things to come, this injustice extends far beyond their expanse, to other resources and other 'elsewheres'. From the deaths of child labourers mining cobalt in the Democratic Republic of Congo to poisoned rivers downstream of lithium sites in Tibet, under capitalism certain areas, ecosystems, and people are necessarily privately enclosed and exploited to sustain the demands and growth of those in wealthier centres.

While enclosure in domains such as intellectual property generates a false scarcity, the ceaseless expansion of unequal accumulation implied by the green capitalist agenda can, by contrast, be understood as generating both a false scarcity (the implicit assumption underlying liberal climate agendas is that 'development' in the Global South threatens to exceed 'planetary boundaries') *as well as* a 'false abundance'. This is an experience of abundance for the global middle and upper classes that is predicated on private control of resources and sinks, reliant on cheap and increasingly unsustainable exploitation of labour and nature to the necessary exclusion of the world's majority. However, scarcity of resources is a social relation, generated by the unequal distributions that private ownership and accumulation sustain and expand; its undoing is the reclamation of these essential resources for the collective, with democratically accountable mechanisms of stewardship allocating them according to need and towards the goal of collective flourishing.

Offsetting Oblivion

In only a few years, the phrase 'net zero' has rocketed from the fringes of the climate science community into a household term. Enshrined in the Paris Climate Agreement and adopted by several national governments, the term – which effectively describes a state in which as much carbon dioxide is emitted as is captured or 'drawn down' by various means – is fraught with controversy. Though a state of 'true zero' emissions is impossible, the widespread uptake of the term has been criticised as a potential Get Out of Jail Free card for governments and companies, enabling them to avoid deep emissions cuts under the implicit assumption that negative emissions technologies and reforestation will one day make up the difference. The adoption of emissions targets is an essential step in reducing them, but the assumptions and strategies underlying a growing number of 'net-zero' pledges are frequently divorced from reality.

High emitters from Shell and BP to Delta Airlines and Heathrow Airport now boast 'net-zero' targets for their operations, and carbon offset schemes are a rapidly expanding multi-billion-dollar industry. Many firms champion the virtues of their 'nature-based solutions' to the climate crisis, forest- and land-use-based offsets that constitute the vast majority of voluntary offset schemes.[20] Nature-based solutions for offsetting take a variety of forms, often portrayed in corporate messaging with picturesque clips of wetland and mangrove forest restoration. However, encouraging and palatable as the phrase 'nature-based' might sound, it belies serious problems, not only with respect to efficacy, but also with the entrenchment of injustice at a global scale. In reality, a carbon offset could take the form of simply paying for a forest not to be destroyed, afforestation – or perhaps nothing at all. As the climate scientist Kevin Anderson has argued, with respect to impacts on emissions, 'offsetting is worse than doing nothing',[21] because it creates the veneer of climate action where none has been taken and, as a consequence, potentially encourages even more harmful activity.

The offsetting industry has been plagued with issues surrounding additionality (in other words, would this have happened anyway?), permanence (planting a forest will accomplish little if it is subsequently razed), and double counting.[22] At the COP25 negotiations, for example, Brazil pushed for leeway in offset accounting, enabling it to count rainforest preservation towards its own carbon targets while

still selling offsets to other countries and entities. The negotiations ended without resolution. There are also serious
questions about temporality: as the UN Environment
Programme acknowledges, trees planted today will not mature
quickly enough to allow us to reach the IPCC's 2030 target
of reducing emissions by 45 percent relative to 2010. And
many are simply deceptions. Towards the end of 2020, it
came to light that several major firms including BlackRock
and JP Morgan had been working with leading environmental NGO the Nature Conservancy to offset their
operations, premised on protecting ecosystems throughout
the United States; the trouble was, the offsets turned out to
be meaningless, promising preservation of areas that were
already protected or not under threat.[23] The gravest concern
with these nature-based solutions, however, is that they will
further cement the expansive inequalities in wealth, power,
and resource use that drive environmental crisis and injustice to begin with.

For companies that can afford them, offsets are a licence
to continue business as usual. In September 2020, French
fossil fuel giant Total sold its first $17 million shipment of
'carbon-neutral' liquified natural gas to CNOOC, the
Chinese state-owned oil producer. The fossil gas was, according to the companies involved in the transaction, fully
'neutralised' by the purchase of a $600,000 offset (roughly
3.5 percent of the value of the sale) which paid members of
a community in Zimbabwe to engage in fire-preventative
forest maintenance. However, experts were quick to deride
the claim of carbon neutrality – based on 'a meager few
dollars' towards conservation – as 'indefensible' and likely
to have, at best, a marginal impact on counteracting the
emissions embodied in the shipment.[24]

Dealings in 'carbon neutral' fossil gas get to the heart of the problem with green capitalism and private, unaccountable, and, critically, profit-driven dominion over the planet's resources, as well as the implications of their use. Global oil and gas giants have provided us with decades of evidence that they are incapable of driving the transition to a decarbonised economy. ExxonMobil, having been one of the first entities to have its scientists affirm the link between carbon emissions and human-caused climate change, subsequently spent decades denying this fact and spreading disinformation to secure continued profits. BP, to deflect from its outsize role in driving accelerating warming and environmental degradation, was the first to popularise the idea of the personal carbon footprint, encouraging consumers to estimate theirs and make small changes to their lives rather than question the viability of the fossil economy. Now, these companies' hollow gestures to the 'energies of the future' amount to little more than branding exercises: in 2019, the fossil fuel industry's investment in renewable and carbon capture technologies represented less than 1 percent of their total capital expenditures. In 2020, amid a crashing oil price and demand shock, this climbed to just 3 percent. Offsetting schemes provide yet another mechanism for continued extraction while creating the impression that these firms are adapting with the times.

In one of the world's largest private-sector commitments to offsetting, Shell pledged in 2019 to spend $100 million per year for three years on nature-based solutions in an effort to reconcile its desire for a green image with its plans to continue expanding oil and gas production for decades to come. Putting aside the fact that the $100 million commitment constituted less than 1 percent of the company's profits that year, a deeper issue stems from the materiality of what this pledge implies. By one estimate, offsetting Shell's own contribution to global emissions would require an area of land nearly the size of England.[25] Shell's highest ambition 'Sky' scenario for decarbonising the global economy implies an area of reforested land the size of Brazil, in large part to compensate for the company's expectations of expanded gas production long into the future. The trouble is, in a world inhabited by more than just Shell, the physical requirements for meeting this widely applauded ambition are farcical. The International Energy Agency, for example, set out a net-zero scenario whose reliance on the massive scaling up of 'bioenergy' (burning organic matter such as forests for energy) will require a landmass the size of India and Pakistan combined simply to house these crops.[26]

Land grabs of this scale are not mere hypotheticals. They are already underway. Between 2002 and 2017, ActionAid found land seizure associated with demand for biofuel crops totalled 17 million hectares, displacing subsistence farmers, Indigenous communities and many other communities in the Global South in the process, often with direct violence and intimidation.[27] Meanwhile, the pivot towards private financing and investment from corporations based in the Global North for 'development' – increasingly under the banner of 'green' development – has often led to 'carbon neocolonialism', whereby land seizures for tree plantations and similar projects to offset the activity of large corporations supplant genuine investment in communities, infrastructure, or adaptation. Because it is often cheaper and easier to undertake these offsets in disadvantaged areas or lower-income countries, this dynamic is in-built to a system of ecological 'conservation' based on markets. In the process, offset schemes routinely undermine advances in the well-being and prosperity of local areas by undercutting or eliminating livelihoods altogether.[28]

In short, nature-based 'solutions' appear anything but. Undoubtedly, extensive reforestation and ecosystem restoration will be a vital part of addressing the climate and nature crises, and are valuable in their own right. Rewilding and the greening of urban spaces will bring countless benefits to biodiversity, public health, and human well-being, as well as cities' capacities to adapt to a warming world. But these actions must be undertaken with a global perspective, and in pursuit of collective human and planetary flourishing – not just as a justification for oil majors to keep drilling. We must not be seduced by the convenience and comfort offered by such schemes, welcoming flashy tree-planting pledges with open arms without considering in whose interests these initiatives are being pursued, and by whom they are controlled. Indeed, the world of carbon offsetting and nature-based solutions is today dominated not by the drive to curb the private accumulation and excessive extraction driving planetary crisis; rather, the proposal is to fight fire with fire, supplementing untenable rates of enclosure and concentrations of wealth and power with yet more private enclosure, stripping power from those who already have little. In place of an urgently needed redistribution of social provision and entitlements to resources, an expansionary green capitalist agenda necessarily sets a course for ever-greater exclusion of swathes of the global population from the fundamentals of a decent life, and sovereignty over how it is lived.

Importantly, although the climate crisis has a tendency to take centre-stage in public discourse as well as policy-making, beyond this carbon-centrism lurk other equally dangerous crises related to the accelerating collapse of eco-systems and biodiversity. Between 1970 and 2014, 60 percent of global wildlife was lost. Today, humans and livestock represent 96 percent of all mammals on Earth. And now, confronted with the collapse of the preconditions for its own reproduction, capitalism is having a long-overdue reckoning with its exploitation of the natural world. Insurance giants and other financial firms have started conducting vast assessments of the value of 'ecosystem services'. In the UK, the landmark 2021 Dasgupta Review on the economics of bio-diversity was received with acclaim for its assessment of the economic value of ecosystems and biodiversity worldwide. Like carbon markets before them, tradable biodiversity cred-its, financial assets, and dedicated markets are springing up backed by influential institutions like the World Economic Forum and World Bank.

Within proposed (and already active) frameworks, financ-ing for biodiversity-related activities can be securitised, with loans bundled up into tradable financial assets meant to better distribute the risks associated with these initiatives, the same sort of financial 'innovation' at the centre of the 2008 financial market crash. At the same time, publicly backed guarantees are being encouraged in major UN-affiliated reports with an eye towards 'shepherding' private capital into these otherwise undesirable investment oppor-tunities – a novel instantiation of what economist Daniela Gabor calls the 'Wall Street Climate Consensus', which saw a massive turn towards publicly guaranteed private invest-ment in development-related projects, effectively socialising risk while privatising return.[29] In many ways, the projects themselves – cordoning off land to plant new forests or paying a landowner not to destroy the wetland on their property – closely resemble those of carbon offsets. They're also marred by the same fundamental pitfall: distilling the immense complexity of natural systems into discrete financial units to be bought and sold for private ownership and use rather than collective benefit.

The concept of 'biodiversity offsetting', for example, has been proposed as a mechanism by which corporations can destroy an ecosystem, provided they offset it with biodiversity of 'equivalent value' elsewhere based on a 'like for like' principle.[30] But according to whom, and to which principles should this 'value' be determined? The absurdity of the approach was exemplified in a recent battle over the proposed felling of the 800-year-old Smithy Wood near Sheffield, UK, to make way for motorway service stations. As compensation, developers proposed an 'offset' of 60,000 new trees somewhere nearby. But an ancient woodland is substantially more than 60,000 trees – it's an immensely complex ecology supporting rich carbon sequestration and providing intrinsic social and cultural value for the community incomparable to a plot of juvenile trees. Moreover, the biodiversity (and the carbon capturing) potential of those 60,000 trees would not be realised for decades – decades that can't be spared at current rates of ecosystem destruction. Thankfully, after years of dedicated local campaigning, the permit for this obscene exchange was revoked.

Ultimately, both carbon offsetting and the assetisation of nature and biodiversity rest on the implicit assumption that the externalities of the market – that is, the harms caused by economic activities for which the perpetrators of the harms do not directly pay – can be 'internalised' through valuation, private ownership, and appropriate pricing. They hinge on the belief that – despite all evidence to the contrary – markets are the most efficient, effective, and fair way to prevent ecological destruction. Moreover, the 'radical uncertainty' of natural systems makes the true risks and costs associated with their loss fundamentally unknowable, even in purely economistic terms.[31] By handing control over the natural commons to the largely unaccountable private authority of powerful firms, we all but guarantee to further cement the economic injustices and dynamics driving the degradation of the climate and environment.

Shell Won't Save Us

The International Energy Agency's recent report on the world's energy future was startlingly clear in its advice for averting catastrophic climate change: we must immediately end all exploration for fossil fuels. Exploiting just the world's known fossil fuel reserves would send us soaring far past a 1.5-degree warmer world and towards a truly unimaginable future. Despite this, fossil fuel giants continue to explore for additional reserves to exploit. Beneath the glossy PR, the world's fossil fuel giants are doing all but nothing to transition their business models to a decarbonised future; from 2015 to 2019, fossil fuels majors' investment in renewables and CCS amounted to an average of less than 0.7 percent of their total capital investment.[32] Despite how much they might proclaim the opposite, fossil fuel firms will not save us.

For years, dedicated legislators and campaigners have sought tirelessly to regulate fossil fuel production and emissions intensity, to little effect. Yet here again, ownership can offer us a potential path forward. Taking the UK's North Sea as an informative example: from the seabed off the coast of the UK, over 1.5 million barrels of oil are extracted every day by dozens of companies.[33] Moreover, despite the UK Oil and Gas Authority's adoption of a 'net zero' commitment, there remains a legally binding requirement for operators to 'maximise economic recovery' of the region's fossil fuel resources, exploiting every cost-effective drop. And at the time of writing, when soaring gas prices in the UK risk driving millions into fuel poverty, BP and Shell have announced bumper profits. Advocates for fracking have seized on the opportunity to suggest that kickstarting the domestic UK shale gas industry could resolve this problem, while ignoring that the UK's private profit-driven oil and gas industry continues to export the vast majority of its product to fetch the best price on the global market.

However, all North Sea and onshore oil resources remain owned by the Crown; the rights to exploit these resources are thus granted by public authority – and could just as easily be withdrawn. Thus, in addition to immediately ceasing new licencing, the government could rescind, renegotiate, or buy producers out of their licences, bringing the seafloor under democratic control for a swift and, critically, just winding-down of production. Critics of a 'nationalise and wind down' approach argue that fossil fuel firms should not be remunerated for these lost assets; there is considerable merit to these arguments, and any remuneration should be calculated to include the harms wrought by fossil fuel production to people and the environment; the cost of decommissioning the infrastructure; the exploitation of underpaid labour in supply chains; and the vast subsidies and bailouts provided to keep extraction profitable and firms afloat. Critics are also apt to point out that the majority of the world's fossil fuel reserves are currently held by state-owned companies;

however, the governance of these companies has little in common with the approach for instilling democratic control and accountability that we advocate: the world's largest state-owned oil companies are those under the control of deeply undemocratic governments, chiefly Saudi Arabia, Iran, and Russia, making the comparison unhelpful.

So long as the world's fossil fuel assets are controlled by corporate actors whose primary goal is the maximisation of profits, our ability to secure a just transition to decarbonised energy at the speed and scale required is put at risk. Put simply, the basic institutional design of the for-profit corporation – when those profits derive overwhelmingly from the extraction and sale of fossil fuels – stands in direct conflict with the demands and time horizons of the climate emergency. Production continues based on prospective profit. So long as producing and exploiting fossil fuels for energy remains profitable – and, critically, more profitable than alternative investment options – energy companies will continue to invest to secure their extraction and sale. As oil prices surge as economies reopen, this remains fatally the case. Shell, for example, recently 'identified no fewer than 21 major oil and gas projects presently under construction, spread across every continent bar Antarctica, and of which 11 would enter production in 2020–21 and 10 in 2022'.[34]

Moreover, a regulate-into-ruin approach – beyond triggering countless lawsuits from corporations arguing discrimination under trade agreements designed to protect their interests – risks devastating fossil fuel workers and the communities which revolve around these industries.[35] When a sharp drop in demand hit oil companies in the pandemic, workers were the first to take the hit, with tens of thousands of jobs shed in the UK and US. Crucially, while there is no place for oil executives in a just transition, there is an essential role for these workers, whose expertise and skills will serve as a vital part of winding down and decommissioning existing fossil fuel production – as well as building the clean energy industries of the future. Democratic public ownership of these firms – subject to stringent terms of accountability and with democratically established timelines and requirements for ending production – would better protect these workers and bring their skills into building a decarbonised economy.

A Return to the First Frontier: What Next?

Land, nature, and their many riches are the original sites of enclosure, the exploitation of which provided the basis for the 'Liberal' properterian ethics of Enlightenment philosophers that continue to inform the rules and structures of global capitalism. Colonial plunder, the expansion of empires, and the forced expulsion of Indigenous peoples – all have been justified by the 'improvement' of supposedly unused land, and all set the stage for an economic system driven by expansion and unending accumulation. Now, as that same system faces existential crisis on a planetary scale, property rights – over land, over the exploitation of nature – are once again the critical fault-line for what comes next. If the question is 'no longer whether to decarbonise, but how',[36] it is these property rights that will determine the contours of the transition to a decarbonised future: towards justice and sustainability, or escalating plunder, violence and exclusion.

The depletion of resources, exploitation of people and nature, and surging production of waste – be it toxic mineral runoff or carbon emissions – are rooted in the highly concentrated, exclusive control over the gifts of this planet. This depletion is intrinsic to capitalism, which demands constant expansion and accumulation to reproduce itself, while generating vast inequalities in wealth and resource use that cannot be sustained. In this sense, planetary boundaries are less a physical absolute than a social construction, with the horizon for surpassing them brought nearer the steeper these inequalities become. The most effective response to mounting ecological crisis, then, is one rooted in democratic principles, liberating nature from the authority of private property and profit. This approach has ethical merit: justice and our basic humanity demand that all life has the opportunity to thrive, and that our flourishing does not require as a precondition the suffering and exploitation of people and nature elsewhere. But for the cynics, a radically democratising agenda for stewardship of the natural world and its resources is also necessary, both politically and physically.

The planet cannot sustain current rates of ecological depletion and carbon emission. However, recent path-breaking research has begun to suggest we can secure a high quality life for all; one study found this remained the case with a population three times larger than we currently have – all with lower energy use.[37] Although calls for slowing birth rates – with their racialised and increasingly fascist undertoness – frequently populate our media, the challenge we face is not runaway population growth, but the profound inequalities and inefficiencies in our economic system, with public provision of, for example, essential services delivering better outcomes and significantly lower resource demands than private alternatives.[38] Our world is one defined by escalating excess for a few, whether the consumption of the wealthy or the destruction wrought with near-impunity by corporations seeking to cut production costs and obstruct environmental regulation. So extreme are these currents that a landmark 2020 review in *Nature Climate Change* affirmed that 'burgeoning consumption has diminished or cancelled out any gains brought about by technological change aimed at reducing environmental impact'.[39] This excess – necessarily to the exclusion of the world's majority – now increasingly undermines the very preconditions for its own maintenance. Upholding a particular mode of living for a particular cohort of the global population has required the exploitation of cheap or free labour, cheap resources, and cheap environmental sinks elsewhere, all of which are finite, and rapidly depleting. As accelerating accumulation by some has been matched by the deepening exclusion and alienation of others – from the fundamentals of life, from political and economic sovereignty – a potent political backlash has grown which threatens the future not only of 'green' capitalism, but of democracy.

To counteract these authoritarian currents, we need a project that will see the Earth's riches returned to the commons, to be stewarded in our collective interest. This is fundamentally a project of democratic and common ownership. In contrast to the widespread idea that the commons is destined for tragedy, common ownership and governance structures continue to prove their remarkable capacity to sustainably and fairly steward nature and resources. This idea is not new. It is, however, conveniently disregarded by seductive appeals to a selfish 'human nature' and the inevitability of current systems of ownership and governance, which serve to uphold existing relations of power – despite the forceful debunking of these claims to inevitability.[40] Moreover, appeals to the efficacy of private self-interest for conserving nature and resources are not borne out by the evidence: a review of more than 80,000 land deals published in *Nature* found that in the vast majority of cases, exclusive purchases – whether made by private companies or foreign governments for exploitation – resulted in accelerated deforestation, significant negative impacts for local communities, and biodiversity loss.[41] The intuitive appeal of 'the tragedy of the commons' tends to be rooted in examples such as depletion of groundwater in the US from industrial agriculture or, saliently, the evisceration of grocery shelves as the pandemic took hold. But these are false comparisons, with the distinctive markings of private corporate interest (intensive agriculture) or, crucially, a lack of governance structure for collective stewardship. The argument for common ownership is not to eliminate governance, but to build it, democratically, such that critical resources can be carefully managed and shared sustainably by all.

Thus, in place of the imperative of 'maximum economic recovery' that currently defines extraction, our resource use should be determined by our collective needs. At the core of this project must be the replacement of private authority over the planet's riches with democratic and common control. There are many alternative models, discussed in the concluding chapter of this book, that can be replicated and scaled to create a natural world that is not exclusively owned and exploited, but stewarded for collective need. Many of these derive from the knowledge of Indigenous communities, who remain the custodians of an incredible 80 percent of global biodiversity, despite representing just 5 percent of the global population.[42] Rather than the 'wisdom' of the market's invisible hand, perhaps this is the wisdom to which we should adhere.

Crucially, this cannot be a project of domestic democratisation and commoning alone. As Thea Riofrancos has documented in *Resource Radicals*, the 'Pink Tide' of socialist governments that swept elections in Latin America at the start of the millennium brought a wave of hope for environmental advocates and Indigenous communities who were hoping to reestablish democratic or collective control over highly contested resources. However, undoing private authority in the context of a global system dominated by US economic interests and hegemonic struggle with China alongside deeply unequal distributions of power in the global economy proved a highly complex task. What emerged in many cases was a reassertion of resource nationalism, and centralised state control over the entitlements to resources.[43]

Now, newly elected progressive governments in countries such as Bolivia and Peru provide a new opportunity to challenge the power of corporate mining interests and the demands of global production, while Chile's election results have given the country its first opportunity to rewrite its dictatorship-era constitution, with significant implications for the stewardship of resources. But just and democratic outcomes are far from determined. The same tensions that in many cases thwarted the hopes for resource democracy and environmental justice during the Pink Tide still remain, and the articulation of 'green recovery' packages by governments in the Global North has spurred predictions of a commodity 'supercycle' that could bring surging demand and corporate exploitation for several years to come. To assuage these tensions, in Latin America and throughout the world, will require a reckoning with global inequalities in wealth and power, ensuring that 'green recoveries' in the US, EU, or UK are not built on the devastation of communities and ecosystems elsewhere.

Conclusion

Owning the Future

The ultimate, hidden truth of the world is that it is something that we make, and could just as easily make differently.
— David Graeber

Across human history, instability has often been seized upon to remake societies. The outcomes, however, have never been certain. Every crisis that has unfolded, and their consequences have been shot through with contingency and political struggle. External shock is not the decisive factor in change, it just creates an opening. The pandemic could constitute a genuinely reconfigurative break akin to the New Deal era, post-war consensus in the UK, or the neoliberal counter-revolution, but what remains to be seen is on whose terms its aftermath will unfold. Can we abolish the relations of private power and profit that have led, time and again, to crisis? Can we build societies of democracy, justice, and freedom?

We need to begin with a much richer conception of democracy, expanding its scope and creating new paths along which it can operate. As author and filmmaker Astra Taylor writes:

The forces of oligarchy have been enabled, in part, by our tendency to accept a highly proscribed notion of democracy, one that limits popular power to the field of electoral politics, ignoring the other institutions and structures (workplaces, prisons, schools, hospitals, the environment, and the economy itself) that shape people's lives.[1]

Justice, meanwhile, can only be realised in a world where everyone has 'broadly equal access to the necessary material and social means to live flourishing lives';[2] without this, appeals to equality of 'opportunity' mean little. And our understanding of freedom must move beyond the prevailing assertion of negative liberty (in other words, 'just let me live' freedom) towards the positive freedom of genuine self- and co-determination – the ability to develop one's capabilities, endeavours, and potential, and bring them to fruition in cooperation, without infringing on the rights and well-being of others or of the natural world. Individual freedom, in other words, should be understood as only possible through collective liberation. This is a much deeper freedom than the form that we enjoy today, in that enjoying it does not, by definition, require the domination of others.

Securing these goals will require that we go beyond piecemeal progressive reforms and towards remaking our institutional frameworks. Three horizons of ambition should guide us as we confront the planetary crisis: the democratisation of production, the decommodification of provision, and the defence of the commons. Importantly, we focus here on the potential for ownership to act as a fulcrum for change; the proposals that follow should therefore be viewed not in isolation but as part of a constellation

of shifts, from a transformative expansion of public investment to a new settlement for labour.

A Democratic Economy

Of labour, by labour, for labour

A democratic economy begins in the corporation, whose
prevailing design, governance, and operation have made it
the site from which much of our economy's sickness –
whether ecological devastation or vaccine apartheid – is
derived. Nonetheless, as has been reiterated throughout this
book, the corporate form also harbours a revolutionary
potential: it is inherently social in its operation; politically
contestable in its legal ordering; and an island of non-market
planning within a market-based economy and society. By
fully socialising the corporation – not just its risk, as we
presently do, but also its governance and its rewards, its
investment decisions and its organisation of work – this
potential could be directed towards meeting genuine needs
and furthering our collective capabilities.

Instead of membership to the corporation's 'legislature'
being allocated through shareholding, companies should be
based on a one-worker, one-vote principle. Those under the
direct rule of the firm should also be reflected in its governance. The board should thus be elected by and from the
workforce, with representation secured for the interests of
workers in the supply and distribution chain. Wider environmental interests should be represented too, with a 'green'
Board member with veto powers where proposed actions
breach safe climate and ecological requirements. Organising
membership based on participation, not share ownership, is

both democratic *and* effective. There is a wealth of evidence of the benefits of genuine participation in enterprise, not least in the experience of the cooperative movement, which provides work to 10 percent of the employed global population.[3] Over time, the corporation could become a democratic community comprising labour and other stakeholders, who would decide collectively on its purpose and strategy. However, these changes should not occur in a vacuum. Instead, they should form part of a democratisation of economic decision-making both within and beyond the firm, from strengthening sectoral collective bargaining, to ensuring workers in multinational corporations have democratic voice in their organisation.

Away with the stock market
The firm cannot be fully democratised unless it is freed from the disciplining force of finance. This implies nothing less than eliminating the stock market as the ruling structure of corporate governance and control. Stock markets, rather than a neutral source of productive capital for firms, are in large part a convenience for the major asset-owning class to trade liquid claims on corporate income. Chronically low interest rates, central bank corporate bond purchasing schemes since the financial crisis, and tax advantages have accelerated a shift in corporate financing strategies from equity to debt, reducing the importance of equity financing while building a record corporate debt bubble.[4] Moreover, while share offerings do raise funds for companies, they amount to far less than is spent in aggregate on share buybacks,[5] and new share issuances are dwarfed by the volume of share trading, underscoring the stock market's true function.[6]

It is now commonplace to argue that shareholder primacy, rather than orienting corporations towards maximum productivity or even efficiency, has served as a remarkably effective force for disciplining companies into disgorging ever more cash to shareholders.[7] While some stewardship-oriented institutional investors try to push companies in more socially and environmentally beneficial directions, the incentives of corporate governance and the nature of ownership under asset manager capitalism structurally undermine the possibility of this 'engagement' reaching critical mass. So, if stock markets are primarily serving as a convenience for rearranging financial claims, and shareholder primacy is simply a vehicle for funnelling firms' cash to shareholders, the question is: What on earth are shareholders for?

One step to transforming how shareholding operates would be to democratise the chain of financial intermediation, giving the underlying beneficiary or owner of the share wealth the final say. Currently, asset managers dominate corporate voting through their control of other peoples' money. Simple but powerful steps could change this. For example, as legal academic Ewan McGaughey argues, the law could insist asset managers only vote on company shares when following instructions from the beneficial owner and ensure that capital funds, like pension trusts, are elected by their members. While an undoubted advance on the present, we must go further for two reasons: first, the internationalisation of shareholding has broken the chain between investors and the community of the firm – it is unclear why such investors should be given such powerful sway over an entity to which they have such a distant and often disinterested relationship. Second, pension entitlements and financial wealth are sharply unevenly held. Democratising voting rights attached to underlying inequalities in ownership would not democratise the firm but rather constitutionalise an undemocratic institution where voting power is accorded based on one's share of wealth, not participation.

There is scant justification for maintaining the entitlement to corporate voting rights still anachronistically attached to public shareholding. Shareholders in public companies are overwhelmingly external to the firm, passive recipients not creators of wealth, and bear little risk. Instead of turning profits over to external shareholders, the company should have genuine stakeholders democratically decide how to distribute its surplus – for example, to reinvest to expand its productive capacities, increase real wages, and enable a managed reduction in working hours without loss of pay. The inviolable right of ownership to dispose of the surplus and the right to manage would give way to a deeper democratic community: work organised on the terms of the workforce. Instead of capital hiring labour, labour would organise capital, and the company would be transformed from an engine of upward redistribution into an institution of shared wealth and voice.

Critics are swift to decry proposals for the democratising of corporate ownership and control rights – such as Bernie Sanders's proposed Employee Ownership Fund, which would gradually distribute a fraction of a corporation's shares to a worker-held trust – as expropriation from the middle class and vulnerable pensioners. But private pensions as a sector are in crisis[8] and seeking ever higher returns to support their growing liabilities, have already begun a decisive shift out of public-listed equity; public equities have fallen from nearly 70 percent of UK pensions' investment in 2003 to a low of just 18 per cent in 2020.[9] UK workers' pension funds now own just 6 percent of UK listed shares and only 8 percent of their total holdings are in UK equity markets; this has substantially weakened the link between dividends and pensions in recent decades. Public policy should simply accelerate the final phase of this shift over time, incentivising the reallocation of private pension wealth towards investment in government and corporate bonds to support a sustained expansion in public investment, or even more targeted investments under a community wealth-building strategy.

More fundamentally, workplace pensions should be reevaluated as the mechanism for providing security in old age – particularly in light of the crisis of pension shortfalls and significant inequalities in pension wealth that currently define global systems. Instead of the current system, which relies on private pension wealth as the main source of security and dignity for retirees – entangling its beneficiaries in market logics and providing a rich source of income for asset managers while failing to provide decent security in old age for all – a universal state pension based on a pay-as-you-go system with a generous replacement rate and a minimum floor should be implemented.[10] This would both reduce pensioner poverty and have the advantage of limiting the structural power of financial markets on the behaviours of older voters.

Rent-extracting shareholders with out-of-date control rights have long ceased to be an essential component of financing what we need and can do. A new network of public banks and strategic financial institutions could instead provide capital for new entrants and the minority of mature firms using the stock market to raise funds for investment. For investors seeking returns, or companies seeking an injection of capital, they could purchase or issue, respectively, a form of shares without control rights attached, not unlike the

'Preference Shares' form already used by many corporations. In the age of asset manager capitalism, it is time the shareholder is dethroned and the democratic company born.

Building a common wealth

The wealth produced by the corporation is enabled by common efforts and inheritance beyond the boundaries of the firm: in the accumulated wealth of society, labour, and nature. An enduring form of economic democracy must therefore see corporate wealth and income drastically redistributed among those who create it, both within and beyond national boundaries. Otherwise, policies to democratise the corporation alone could simply reproduce inequalities, privileging workers in frontier firms (the most productive and typically largest firms in a given sector) while disadvantaging those sectors and firms that, while less valuable under today's profit-based metrics, are nonetheless truly vital to human and environmental well-being.

To address these challenges, from James Meade, the theorist of liberal socialism, we can rescue the idea of a social wealth fund. Acting as a vehicle for collective wealth holding, this fund could purchase corporate bonds via public sector debt-financed acquisition of assets or be granted income rights in large companies as part of a new social settlement. Strengthening the public balance sheet, after decades in which it has been run down, the fund would act as a counter against the inequality-intensifying consequences of existing, unequal patterns of corporate ownership.

The fund could serve as an anchor in the transition to a distinctly more democratic economic settlement: over time, a broad share of income currently monopolised by corporate shareholders would be redistributed, progressively socialising the corporate form while mechanically reducing the concentration of private wealth. In totality, these measures would challenge the fundamental role of ownership in capitalist relations: the surplus would be politically determined not market allocated; the purpose and nature of enterprise would be democratically negotiated; and working life organised around freely chosen goals and practices, not a social relationship founded on domination and wealth extraction from waged labour to capital.[11]

At the same time, we also need to raise the profile and capacity of alternative models of ownership. A rich variety of forms are already building the democratic economy, from the cooperative movement, which already combines democratic ownership with inclusive governance of the workplace, to community development financial institutions that create and broaden economic opportunities in neighbourhoods that have experienced historical disinvestment. Community wealth-building strategies that nurture locally oriented and inclusive business models are also on the rise, and from Preston to Cleveland, Kerala to Kigama, an alternative future is being incubated in the present. The challenge – and opportunity – is to scale and systematise these examples, which currently operate in a hostile economic environment, into a genuinely pluralistic economy.

The Decommodified Life

Solid foundations

Democratisation of production must be matched by the decommodification of life's essentials. As Covid-19 painfully confirmed, the dominance of market relations means too few people have guaranteed access to the services and resources for a secure, dignified, and free life. This inequality – rooted in underlying inequalities in ownership of the means of (re) production – sets in train processes of exploitation and expropriation. To borrow the choice words of a recent Fox News guest discussing unemployment benefits, 'a hungry dog is an obedient dog'; in other words, market dependency is a highly effective tool for keeping workers under capital's heel.[12] By contrast, from material security springs genuine autonomy. With a decent standard of living guaranteed through social provision of life's necessities, and a welfare system that guarantees a living income floor for all, people would be free to work through choice rather than compulsion.

Two complementary policies can help free us from this dependency: the provision of universal basic services (UBS), and the extension of twenty-first century models of democratic public ownership. While a wide array of services have been suggested by different advocates of UBS, we propose beginning with key elements of what has been termed the foundational economy, 'those goods and services consumed by all (regardless of income and status) because they support everyday life'.[13] Following the Manchester University Centre for Research on Socio-Cultural Change, this could begin with areas like utilities, transport, nutrition, and health and social care.[14] Not by coincidence, these were the vital sectors acutely exposed to Covid-19, employing the 'key workers' who we have been collectively most reliant upon during the pandemic (and throughout our lives).

Concretely, three areas emerged as acute fault-lines in the pandemic that require urgent transformation: infrastructures of care, full fibre broadband access, and housing and land ownership. While hardly an exhaustive list, these areas offer illustrative examples of how decommodified social provision, democratically organised and resourced, can unpick privatised ownership-related patterns of exclusion and inefficiency and build societies of genuine security and equity.

Centring care

The crisis in care cannot be solved by transformations in ownership alone; our society is scarred by a long-standing devaluation of this essential form of labour which merits a much richer discussion than we can manage here. Ownership can, however, offer a potentially transformative tool for the professional care sector, which has been so decimated by financialised logics and investor control. There are a range of models that could replace extractive investor ownership and address the current prioritisation of cost-cutting and 'productivity'. Proposals like the Scottish government's National Care Service contain the seeds of a public care infrastructure in the vein of public health systems and other social infrastructures, while conducive tax and regulatory conditions could scale up cooperatively owned care provision.[15] In Italy, for instance, favourably designed conditions have supported the growth of thousands of cooperative welfare services providing for up to 5 million recipients.[16] To that end, the liquidity-providing power of central bank institutions should be directed to support non-profit care providers, allowing them to operate beyond the discipline of financial markets and control of for-profit investors.

Broadband communism

In the 2019 UK general election, the Labour Party's proposal to build a publicly owned full fibre network was ridiculed as 'broadband communism'. This derision both naturalised the failures of actually existing 'broadband capitalism' – under-investment in remote communities amid redundant overcapacity in city centres, digital redlining, and a focus on financial extraction over network delivery – and missed the point: delivering a universal infrastructure is most equitably and efficiently done through democratic planning and investment, not financialised competition. The stark digital divide so painfully evident during the pandemic would be best addressed by building a publicly owned full fibre broadband network that can provide connection free at the point of use as a twenty-first century right. Instead of leaving its development to the prerogatives and time horizons of commercial actors, we should learn from how previous nationwide infrastructures like railways, telephones, and roads were developed: as projects of developmental, modernising states that prioritised universality, equity, and efficiency over returns to shareholders.

Housing security for all

Home ownership is a structuring force of the asset economy. There are a host of proposals to tackle its power, but ultimately the goal should be the guarantee of decent, secure, and beautiful housing for all regardless of whether one owns their home.

In reality, a blended approach is likely necessary to achieve this: expanding in tandem the supply of publicly owned homes for social rent and affordable private ownership; challenging credit-based drivers of house-price inflation while mediating that process fairly; democratising planning to ensure quality and sustainability of housing and built environments, not just quantity. This is a formidable task that faces several obstacles: in Berlin, for example, where long-standing stable rents have given way to soaring costs in recent years amid expanding 'housing as asset class' investor ownership, the efforts of renters' unions have faced an uphill battle. A successful city-wide referendum to impose rent caps was later struck down by the German courts, while professional investors continue to fight tooth and nail against proposals to buy back hundreds of thousands of formerly public housing units.[17] Thus, in economies marked by widespread but not universal home ownership, achieving progress on housing security will require sensitively building a coalition of renters and asset owners behind an agenda that ensures everyone has a safe and secure place to live and be, regardless of whether they own housing wealth, rather than treating the home as an object of accumulation.

The return of public ownership

Beyond these sectors, decommodifying the foundations of life means reembracing democratic public ownership. There are many spheres in which the fundamentals of a good life are compromised by the prerogatives of commercial provision, stymying investment where it's needed and creating unsustainable inefficiencies with damaging impacts both within and beyond borders. Recognition of the need for systemic change is stirring. The Transnational Institute has tracked almost 1,000 recent re-municipalisations across the world as communities – from Paris's water network to new public telecommunication services in Chattanooga – have reclaimed essential services from private operators, bringing their delivery back into the public sphere.[18] Just as public ownership and investment helped build the infrastructure and technologies of the twentieth-century economy, from electrification to transport, so it should play a central role in creating the conditions for a post-carbon world.

Shielded from the imperative of maximising returns and shareholder demands, publicly owned enterprise can drive economic, social, and ecological transformation by undertaking the riskier innovation and less immediately profitable provision (for instance servicing remote communities, driving more ambitious climate strategies, or reclaiming resources for local use) that the private sector is both failing and unwilling to deliver. It can also more effectively coordinate action at scale, which is a fatal flaw in the private sector's response to planetary crisis. At the same time, governance must adapt to the twenty-first century: it must differ from top-down, managerial forms of public ownership that were excessively centralising and undemocratic, embracing management and decision-making processes that value the knowledge of workers, users, and citizens.[19]

Equality as ecology
Decommodifying the foundational economy is also essential to erode the profound inequalities of wealth, power, and consumption currently driving the environmental and climate crisis. Environmental advocates are fond of referencing 'Earth Overshoot Day' – the day each year on which the global population surpasses the amount of resources that can sustainably be consumed in a given year. But contrary to the reactionary narratives this often supports – that there are 'too many' humans for the Earth to handle, or that economic 'development' and birth rates in the Global South are driving us to ruin – the limits against which we are pressing are not simply 'natural' or 'planetary', but

overwhelmingly the product of social relations and political settlements, which can and must be replaced.

A small fraction of the global population is responsible for the vast majority of energy and resource consumption. The average citizen of the UK will have been responsible for more carbon emissions in just two weeks than someone living in Rwanda or Ethiopia will in a whole year, and produces 200 times the climate emissions of the average Congolese person; in the US it is 585 times as much.[20] But evidence also shows the world is capable of supporting a population three times as large as we currently have with just 60 percent of the energy we currently consume.[21] The obstacle to a world of universal abundance, dignity, and freedom is therefore not physical, but relational. The good news: this means we can overcome it. But it also means that any commitment to decommodifying the fundamentals of a decent life requires a global perspective to be realised. Indeed, the freedom of a 'universal' abundance that is contained within borders and requires the domination and exploitation of others, is no freedom at all.

Defending the Commons

Common knowledge

Technology is our common inheritance. Over generations of collective endeavour, we have created the technical possibilities for us all to enjoy lives of greater freedom and security. The extraordinary speed of the development of the Covid-19 vaccine is a testament to this remarkable innovative capacity. Too often, however, the liberatory potential contained within technical systems is hindered by the legally enforced enclosure of technology and its spoils, and by the direction of investment based on imperatives of private accumulation. A break with the institutions of private ownership and investment that presently corral and limit human knowledge is long overdue; in their place, we can build a flourishing technological commons.

Perhaps most immediately pressing in this respect are steps towards commoning intellectual property (IP). As conditions of vaccine apartheid amid a global public health emergency made clear, existing approaches to IP threaten the safety and livelihoods of millions of people around the world. This is not an aberration. Rather, it reflects a system in which knowledge created through public investment or support is quickly enclosed at a global scale by legal regimes that create exclusive rights to use – and consequently to profit. False scarcity imposed by the enclosure – exclusion dynamic currently enables rent extraction on a vast scale at a terrible cost to human life, well-being, and capability.

At the same time, the climate and public health emergencies demand a transformative increase in public investment focused on addressing the intersecting economic, social, and ecological crises we now face. Currently, new technologies are developed mainly in order to expand market share, control, and accumulation, not to free humanity from drudgery or expand our capabilities. As David Graeber once asked: Where are the flying cars we were promised? Though perhaps tongue-in-cheek, the question contains a firm kernel of truth: Why haven't we created the world of technological wonder envisioned in the science fiction of the twentieth century? His answer (and ours) is that the imperatives of profit making and capital accumulation have produced a system in which the security of private property is a chief concern (hence our tremendous investment in the technologies of war and defence), while the technology to liberate humankind from drudgery is not needed, as there will always be people desperate to perform it to achieve basic security.[22] Changing this – rapidly developing and adopting pro-labour, decarbonised technologies and technical systems – means decoupling investment in innovation from the profit imperative and private monopolisation of allocation. Given the urgency of the climate and nature crises, the need – 'to let our imaginations once again become a material force in human history',[23] – is immense.

Data socialism

If knowledge is power, data is its source, providing the raw material for automating technologies. Rather than enabling important and socially generated data to be enclosed for private ends, any project capable of securing post-scarcity conditions will harness data's inherently social quality to plan to meet needs. For instance, data could be commoned through a network of 'data trusts', such as those established in municipalist cities including Barcelona and Amsterdam, used to enhance low-carbon mobility and public health. These autonomous legal bodies would act as custodians and stewards of specific data sets, providing residents, workers, and organisations with access to and democratic control over data that could improve their lives, enabling us to move beyond inequality-generating models of city growth and development.

At the same time, however, we should resist the data panopticon. There are certain things that should never be a target for the extraction, analysis, and use of data. Instead, we need new ways of deciding whether to collect data in the first place, and how it should be used, rather than leaving these decisions in the hands of private corporations and weakly unaccountable state apparatuses. Building a genuine data commons therefore implies leaving some data 'in the ground', determined through collective deliberation.

Return to Eden

Though carbon emissions and their catastrophic effects have dominated the public debate on the state of our planet, a changing climate is only one piece of the puzzle; biodiversity loss and the collapse of ecosystems (intimately related to rising global temperatures) are as much a risk to humankind. Land and nature are the original sites of enclosure. What was once a commonly shared resource has been parcelled up for private benefit to the exclusion of the world's vast majority. Now, nature is once again becoming the frontier for expansion and enclosure, with offset markets and financial constructions striving to segment its complexity into tidy, tradable assets.

The agenda for converting what remains of the commons, nature, and biodiversity into tradable financial assets is marching swiftly forward. From the United Nations to the World Bank and an array of private investment summits, the hunger for markets in 'ecosystem services' and 'biodiversity offsets' is immense. In a market-based society, so the logic goes, nature is worth nothing unless it has a price; by enabling private investors and corporations to trade the destruction of a mature wetland for a freshly planted mono-species forest of equivalent financial 'value' somewhere else in the world, we can conserve biodiversity, the carbon cycle, water systems, and beyond. In this view, man is inherently selfish, collective stewardship untenable, and private interest the only route to preservation.

However, the reverse has repeatedly proved true. In the Brazilian Amazon, where land invasions surged 135 percent in 2019 alone,[24] forests within the territories of Indigenous communities with full collective governance rights show deforestation 'significant orders of magnitude' lower than areas even immediately outside the territory.[25] Importantly, more than 2 million hectares of Brazilian Amazon remain only partially under the collective governance of the Indigenous communities living there; fraught political processes have denied them certain key rights over these territories. This is first and foremost an indefensible injustice; it is also to the detriment of the forest's health. In Peru, granting land titles to Indigenous communities led to almost immediate reductions in forest clearance and ecosystem disturbances. And in Mexico, the state-supported establishment of community forest trusts has created a large and highly effective system of stewardship which has seen communities balance their use of forest resources with long-term conservation.[26]

Agriculture, too, has been shown to benefit from collective governance and stewardship: from trials of community land management in Germany[27] to enduring legacies of 'agro-ecological' smallhold farming in the Global South, shifts away from ultra-intensive, soil eroding, and dispossessing industrial agriculture have the potential to secure a food system that is 'carbon-dioxide-absorbing, biodiversity defending, and resilient in the face of climate change', while producing more per land unit than industrial agriculture.[28] There are proposals at hand for how these forms of governance could work even in a country with as much large-scale private ownership as the UK; for instance, the 'Public Commons Partnership', proposed by academics Keir Milburn,

Kai Heron, and Bertie Russell, offers a blueprint for the public sector to support community stewardship of assets, including land, developing new democratic subjectivities in the process.[29]

The evidence in favour of collective, sovereign governance and stewardship of land and natural commons is striking but should come as no surprise. Indigenous communities have managed land in the collective interest throughout history, and as a result they remain the stewards of an astonishing 80 percent of the world's biodiversity, despite representing just 5 percent of the human population.[30] Indigenous sovereignty should be respected and extended, in the vein of the Land Back movement, as a matter of justice – not as a crude tool to serve someone else's ecological aims. In stewarding all of Earth's remaining ecological diversity, these should be the models of stewardship and governance which we emulate. The so-called 'tragedy of the commons' is a misconstrual; private control and exploitation of resources continues to deliver the real tragedy.[31] The clarion call of market-based mechanisms must therefore be resisted, and the rights to land and vital resources restored to forms of public, community, and common governance.

Shell won't save us: Reprise

Finding our way out of the fossil fuel economy is a life-and-death task for humanity. We are up against the extraordinary rights fossil fuel firms have been granted in determining the future of the planet – powers they have thus far used to enrich themselves and shareholders while deceiving the public about the damage they've wrought in doing so. Fortunately, these rights are publicly granted through the protections of private property law, and are therefore

contestable and subject to change. Courts are already beginning to recognise this. Multiple rulings in domestic judiciaries
against fossil fuel companies have weighed the relative rights
afforded to private property versus human life, and found –
in a decisive break with the history of Anglo-American
capitalism – that human life is worth more. In this sense,
regulation to prevent fossil fuel extraction is as much a
change in private property rights as public ownership. Rather
than formally taking the assets under its management, the
state has simply removed part of a private firm's rights to
do with its property as it will. Regulation that is demand-
ing enough to end fossil fuel extraction at the pace and
scale the climate crisis demands will, ultimately, not be very
different from public ownership as a tool to constrain extraction. Whichever path is taken, it must be one in which the
dominion of private property is no longer asserted above
the needs of human and non-human life, and it must be
taken swiftly.

There are, admittedly, few immediate examples to draw
on in this respect, in large part because fossil fuels remain
so deeply imbricated in every aspect of our lives. However,
bold ideas have begun to emerge which propose bringing
domestic fossil fuel producers into public ownership, for
example in the United States by using the Federal Reserve's
existing legal power to 'buy and sell financial assets to
regulate systemic risk'.[32] Given the existential risk of continued fossil fuel exploration and production, utilising this
power is eminently reasonable. Moreover, throughout the
pandemic's economic rupture, countless fossil fuel companies
entered financial difficulty owing to their fragile balance
sheets and sought public assistance. These crisis moments
are not unique to global pandemics; rather, 'history shows

these are systemic cycles of a privately owned fossil fuel industry – features, not bugs'.[33] Rather than occurring in cycles, and providing no-strings-attached relief for corporate executives and shareholders, bailouts should support workers, people, and planet; to achieve this, states should utilise bailout negotiations to take controlling stakes in companies, for instance through debt-to-equity mechanisms, giving them publicly accountable control over their operations.

There is no silver bullet for overcoming the use of fossil fuels as an energy source. Our approach is one of pragmatism, and of bringing under democratic control those reserves that do lie within our purview. Sudden and sweeping legislation that can bring the fossil fuel industry in line with a 1.5 °C world is likely to result in years of trade agreement disputes. Domestic court rulings in favour of binding emissions reductions as in the Dutch case against Shell, despite providing piercing moments of hope, are similarly beleaguered by extensive appeals processes and loopholes to be exploited by the corporations involved. Waiting for these resolutions is time we do not have to spare.

Securing post-carbon prosperity will require more than fairly winding down fossil fuel production and consumption. We must simultaneously rapidly scale a fair and clean energy future for all. If the energy profile of fossil fuels – a stock that lends itself to privatised control and concentrated ownership[34] – underpins carbon capitalism and all the unequal and hierarchical relationships this entrains, then the flow of wind, wave, and solar power points in a radically different direction: towards collective management and democratic planning, the communal stewardship of shared renewable resources, and the abundance of a nurtured commons. Decentralised, decarbonised, and democratically guided, a clean energy future will be best secured on foundations of common ownership and governance that are radically distinct to the institutional arrangements that undergirded the carbon empire.

From Atacama to Yangtze: Sacrifice zones and 'green' capitalism

Fossil fuels are profoundly imbricated in our lives, and continue to be a source of immense power and wealth for a select few. Replacing them is therefore a complex political – not just technological – challenge. This struggle is currently tilted in favour of escalating extraction from sacrifice zones and populations to sustain the demands of our unequal global economy, evidenced by the explosive growth of the EV and lithium battery industries, and the simultaneous expansion of offset schemes. Both these processes necessitate enormous enclosure of land and resources to serve the interests of wealthy economies. From the salt flats of the Atacama to the poisoned Yangtze River, a transition to a decarbonised society that is predicated on the 'greening' of capitalism and minimising disruption to the existing global economy has already decided on a differential valuation of human lives.

Rejecting this valuation will hinge on undoing the global inequalities in wealth and power that grow from and define global capitalism. Thus, tackling the climate and nature crises requires us to ask: If we value human (and non-human life), and if we believe in freedom, justice, and equality, what are we willing to change? The glossy 'ecological modernisation' of European technocracy and techno-optimism of the emerging US and UK climate agendas – which foresee a future of unchanged economic and social relations defined by carbon capture, sprawling renewable expansion to sustain current energy demands, and one-to-one replacement of our cars for EVs – belie vast quantities of material throughput and resource extraction. They also conceal, beneath the promise of green products and 'carbon-neutral flights' an enormous and growing demand for offset schemes which would enclose huge swathes of land, often through extensive land grabs.

Any agenda which takes justice seriously, then, will also take seriously demands for radical redistribution of ownership, wealth, and power in the global economy. Scholars of racial justice have set out the case for climate reparations – payments owed by wealthy nations to the poorer countries from which they have systematically extracted wealth for centuries, and who are on the frontlines of a climate and environmental catastrophe they largely did not create. This could take the form of green technology transfers and Trade-related Intellectual Property Rights (TRIPS) waivers – but it also, in all likelihood, will require convergence in wealth within and between countries. Reparations could also take the form of direct cash payments for climate-related loss and damage experienced by poorer nations who have contributed little to environmental damage.[35]

There are also historical models such as the Yasuní-ITT initiative, which proposed an exchange whereby Ecuador would suspend oil extraction in a portion of the Yasuní national park in return for payments of just US $3.6 billion – half of the estimated value if the oil were exploited. Though initially well received, the initiative hit a handful of stumbling blocks including, critically, the failure of the international community to deliver on its already insufficient commitment, with just over $13 million paid. Despite its failure, the initiative offers a potential model from which to base a just mechanism for reducing resource exploitation – overwhelmingly to meet the demands of wealthy nations – in lower-income economies, without leaving those communities high and dry.

Building systems of just and collective stewardship will also require a comprehensive restructuring of core capitalist institutions such as free trade agreements, which overwhelmingly favour the interests of private capital. Indeed, private owners are often equipped with substantially more structural power than even the governments of countries from which they extract resources. This reality was grimly underscored when Exxon lobbyists were caught celebrating the gifts the Trump administration had granted them by securing an Investor-State Dispute Settlement Mechanism (ISDS) in the US–Mexico–Canada Agreement (NAFTA 2.0).

Finally, as governments throughout the world cohere under the banner of 'green recoveries', we must demand that decarbonisation programmes in the capitalist centres are focused on providing decommodified public abundance and collective well-being, rather than 'greening' the atomistic, private property–dominated, and energy- and resource-intensive life we presently live. Anything less would be to commit to a climate apartheid, in which the lifestyles of some are preserved at the deadly exclusion of the world's majority. Fundamentally, efforts for environmental justice must be planetary in perspective, or it is not justice at all. Preserving the beauty of the Nevada desert cannot come at the devastation of the Atacama or the death of the Yangtze – nor, crucially, the exploitation of the people who inhabit and depend on them.

On Strategy

The primacy of property was established through a state-led political agenda that did not just privatise and outsource but used fiscal and monetary policy to prioritise and inflate the wealth of asset owners. Reversing this will be critical to reshaping the role of ownership in our societies. We can start by taxing wealth over labour income. In doing so, we make certain property claims temporary; as Thomas Piketty argues, 'the wealthiest private owners must return part of what they own to the community every year to facilitate circulation of wealth and reduce the concentration of private property and economic power.'[36] Macroeconomic policy will be fundamental to structural reorganisation based on ownership. This is a political challenge above all. In the shadow of the pandemic and confronting the demands of the climate and nature crisis, there is much we can do with the tools at hand – the coordination of fiscal and monetary policy and sustained public investment – and still more we can afford. Indeed, relative inaction is far, far costlier in all dimensions. The policies we need, both old and new, are known to us. Against our compounding crises of inequality and climate, the need is clear: Democratise the economy, decommodify life, defend the commons!

On radicalism versus reformism

For any of this to happen, it will depend on a comprehensive restructuring – indeed reimagining – in our property relations. Shifts of this scale can be precipitated in a variety of forms, as Rosa Luxemburg (writing now over a century ago) argued. Political and economic reforms – while not sufficient to bring about a full and enduring social and economic transformation on their own – are nonetheless necessary tools in the struggle to do so, providing opportunities to ignite political consciousness, hone the skills of political organisation and management, and build the breadth of coalition necessary to deliver lasting change.[37] As Luxemburg wrote,

> Legislative reform and revolution are not different methods of historic development that can be picked out from the counter of history, just as one chooses hot or cold sausages. Legislative reform and revolution are different *factors* in the development of class society. They condition and complement each other, and are at the same time reciprocally exclusive.

The proposals we've offered throughout this book are at various times reformist or revolutionary in their orientation, with several falling somewhere in between. Importantly, our proposals for near-term legislative and policy reforms that operate within existing institutions cannot and should not be thought of as goals in and of themselves, but as constituting a (necessarily incomplete) strategy towards building a more transformational politics. Not only do they prefigure the kinds of changes that define our vision for a more free, democratic, equal, and sustainable world, giving tangible demonstrations of how life could be ordered differently, but they also help build the necessary coalitions, or 'historic bloc', across society, uniting diverse groups behind a shared vision and enlisting their agency within the institutions in which they move, whether workers in the firm, carers in the household, or renters in a housing union.[38]

Nonetheless, while institutional reordering is essential to building a coalition, a series of legislative and institutional reforms on their own are not sufficient – nor can we view transformation as merely an incremental march towards some eventual goal. Rather, at all times we must be guided by a much more expansive and necessarily internationalist vision. We need to secure not just worker governance in the corporation, but democratic ownership, participation, and control throughout the whole economy; not simply to end Wall Street domination, but to commit to a world in which everyone has access to the fundamentals for a good life; and not just to establish new protected areas or rewild within our borders, but to recognise that genuine and enduring ecological sustainability means the end of the imperial monopolisation of natural resources and sinks which sustain the mode of living in the Global North through the domination of those 'elsewhere'.[39]

Though hardly an emissary for the wisdom of Rosa Luxemburg, Margaret Thatcher recognised the utility of incremental reforms alongside a revolutionary vision, both prefiguring more radical changes and building a decisively durable new electoral coalition through measures such as the Right to Buy initiative and her sweeping privatisation agenda matched to her brand of authoritarian populism. To break with the economic consensus that has reigned since the neoliberal revolution, even as it continues to destabilise and mutate, we should learn from its strategic successes. The urgent question, then, is how to combine the need for action today (and a recognition that for many, even moderate reforms can mean an end to suffering in the immediate term), with an unwavering commitment to shared principles and a revolutionary spirit that refuses to be co-opted by those whose vision of 'progress' is simply a tamer, kinder capitalism. Central to this question is how to use, transform, or move beyond the state apparatus.

Questions on the state

The state is an often uncomfortable point of discussion for an agenda of democracy, justice, and freedom, inasmuch as, to borrow from James C. Scott, it is a 'vexed institution that is both the ground of our freedoms and our unfreedoms'.[40] We cannot secure the conditions of post-scarcity and expand the realm of true freedom without the coordinating power of a genuinely democratised state. Nor can we challenge concentrated corporate power or act with the urgency and ambition the climate crisis demands. At the same time, the state is a force of violence and unfreedom, of exclusion and control – an institution that defines the boundaries of human worth and expendability, and enforces the primacy of property and capital.

If it contains transformative potential, it also risks anaesthetising an emancipatory politics, sapping the energy of movements, or worse, actively reproducing and extending the injustices of racial capitalism. However, despite its pitfalls and limitations, the reconfiguring and coordinating power of the state is undeniably vital to securing the programme outlined in the preceding chapters: through its control of the force of law, its resource mobilising capacity, its coordinating force. These contradictions and tensions reflect the fact that the state is not a monolithic unified apparatus – it is an ensemble of apparatuses that must be contested and transformed. Our approach to it must therefore reflect this. It is, as the political sociologist Nicos Poulantzas argued, 'neither a thing-instrument that may be taken away, nor a fortress that may be penetrated by means of a wooden horse, nor yet a safe that may be cracked by a burglary'.[41]

We require a plan for contesting and transforming the uneven terrain of the state that relies neither on narrow reformism nor on waiting for a revolution that, if it ever comes, has no guarantee of being democratic. It should not be the horizon of our ambition, but our ambition will depend on mobilising its directive force. This will depend on our ability – through movements, through organising, through culture, through the party form – to democratise the state and use its power to unpick the hierarchies state power has itself erected, while not letting our gaze be consumed by it. This balancing act will only be possible if the left can construct a new historic bloc that is led by and in labour's interest, one that recognises the political complexities of the 'asset economy' while being committed to overturning the primacy of property.

The constituent groups of this historic bloc are emerging, if not already formed: the 'key workers', waged and unwaged, who have kept us safe and society functioning during the crisis; a time-pressed and insecure working-class majority and a growing, precarious 'professional managerial class' whose interests substantively align;[42] social forces driving entwined struggles against racial capitalism, white supremacy, and state oppression; a growing, multi-racial, feminised labour movement; the intersecting needs of renters and financially squeezed debtors everywhere; retirees seeking dignity and security in old age; places and communities on the frontline of disinvestment, deindustrialisation, and environmental harms; emergent cultural energies that draw strength from diversity; businesses nurturing today the democratic economy of tomorrow; and all the organisations, enterprises, and people committed to systemic change as the only safe response to a climate emergency rooted in five centuries of enclosure and extraction.

The elements of this coalition exist. It is found in all those seeking the genuine security, freedom, and dignity that our current political-economic structures systematically deny them. What is required is their organisation and political articulation. Importantly, doing so means confronting perhaps the greatest political challenge facing the left: the imbrication of millions, through the modest expansion of financial wealth and the much broader extension of home ownership over successive generations, into the logics and interests of the wealthiest asset-owning class. The asset economy defines the conjuncture. We cannot wish it away or assume it will unravel. We must attend unswervingly to all its complexity if we are to navigate the changing landscape. But untangling this web is possible: the interest of the majority of small-scale asset owners, both homeowners and pensioners, lies with the even greater majority whose lives are defined by their relative lack of asset ownership and reliance on selling their labour power to live, rather than with the uppermost echelons of the wealthy and powerful. What is clear, though, is that without this disentanglement, there will be no transformative coalition. To that end, we suggest three areas of strategic focus and approach from which we can begin to unite a disorganised majority and build durable, transformative power.

First, as Hall noted: 'Politics does not reflect majorities, it constructs them.'[43] We can't wait expectantly for material conditions to yield up a politics of transformation. Instead, by recognising that identities are never static but politically shaped and reconstituted, we must start fashioning parties, institutions, and movements that can actively organise and politically animate those interests – overcoming the corrosive anti-political and atomistic impulse that neoliberalism has nurtured. We must be both horizontal and vertical, vanguard and broad-based, digitally networked and physically present, in communities, workplaces, and ordinary culture.[44] We must recognise the power of story and myth, not just logic and argument. Forging commonality out of difference, welding social, economic, and cultural forces together, it is critical we stress shared interests not just values; about how, if we apply ourselves, we can consciously transform the world for the better. One critical means of doing so is through prefiguration. From struggles over housing rights to campaigns around the revival of the High Street based on new purposes and ownership models; from digital cooperatives to community wealth building; from Indigenous resistance to extractive industry to community land buyouts and stewardship; we can begin to prefigure wider systemic change through building up even the smallest institutions of the democratic economy. In doing so, even when out of power at a national level, we can demonstrate how collective action can address shared problems, build social power and capacity, and create a new common sense that reframes how we understand the world around us. The radical can be made reasonable.

Second, we must link together efforts to abolish the exploitation of wage-earners *and* the expropriation of the wealth of social and ecological reproduction that is its precondition. They share a common goal: the ability to live freer, richer lives absent the domination and harms produced by properterian logics. They also share a common resolution: denaturalising the primacy of property and the social and economic relations it entrains. That commonality will not, however, inevitably produce a political force capable of transcending the institutional arrangements of the crisis-ridden present; that must be actively cohered and change struggled for and won.

Third, in an era of compounding crises, where a defence of the status quo is a guarantee of accelerating environmental breakdown and social pain, our politics must be abolitionist. Clearly, we must urgently abolish the prerogatives of fossil capital. But this task, existential and world-reshaping as it is, is not enough. In doing so, we must also dismantle, as Alyssa Battistoni writes, the 'social order built around it, from racially segregated suburbs to differential exposure to climate disaster'.[45] The energy transition, in other words, must conjoin abolitionist struggles everywhere: against the extractivism, dispossession, and racialised harms of the Carbon Empire and the oppressive state apparatuses that maintain and defend its power.[46] There are many threads that such an agenda can draw on and be led by, from the abolitionist democracy of Black radical tradition to its contemporary heirs, the global Black Lives Matter movement and coalitions advocating climate reparations, to the Red Deal, which calls for 'directing the coercive capacity of the state away from people and against fossil capital'.[47] But as Ruth Wilson Gilmore argues, this is not an agenda of destruction; instead, 'abolition is a fleshy and material presence of social life lived differently.'[48] It is present in all the ways we build a future still fragile and half-formed, but within reach.

A world to win

The transience of our lives makes freedom the essential goal of political struggle. The freedom of some cannot be based on the exploitation of others, nor exercised through unjustifiable hierarchical relations. It is, therefore, incompatible with the private regimes of power that capitalist property relations generate. Instead, freedom is a shared project: individual liberty secured through collective emancipation. Fundamental to this must be a politics committed to reimagining our systems of ownership and control.

There is no single party, tradition, or movement that can or should do this alone. We need a mass popular front that spans diverse groups. The story that needs to be told is clear: the extraordinary potential of the many is held back by the institutions that shape our lives and communities, an institutional configuration that consolidates wealth and power while inflicting violence on communities and the natural world by prioritising property at the expense of urgent needs. The political right exists to robustly defend and reproduce this configuration; to overcome it, a new bloc must contest and reimagine institutions of ownership and control to fashion an alternative, inclusive, and thoroughly democratic economy and society.

Though not a panacea, building agency and democratic control into every sphere of life can help counter the justified disillusionment with the political system and its agents that many across the political spectrum feel. Above all, to win, we urgently need to move from a moral critique of the present to a sharper political register – not just opposing injustice and inequality in name and through vague gesture but standing and acting explicitly against the forces and institutions that generate these with a compelling, credible plan for dismantling them and erecting in their place a new settlement. As we look to the challenging road leading out of the trauma of Covid-19, this is an object worthy of our collective efforts. It's time we owned the future.

Acknowledgements

Thanks are due first and foremost to Leo Hollis for helping shape the story this book became, and to John Merrick, whose talents as an editor and writer are exceeded only by his generosity and support as a friend and nets companion. To the team at Common Wealth – Miriam Brett, Amelia Horgan, Arby Hisenaj, and Josh Gabert-Doyon – thank you for your patience and for picking up all sorts of loose ends when we descended down the writing rabbit hole. It's a joy to work with and learn from all of you.

From Adrienne, endless thanks to the community who supported and fed me during those very strange locked-down months when this was written – Adam Rutledge, Tilly Cook, Victoria Foing, Alexa Waud, Akinola Davies, Danny Magill, and Mark Juhas. Special thanks to Charlotte Butler for her invaluable feedback, and to Ben Braun, whose intellectual generosity and insights have strongly shaped my thinking. Immense love and gratitude are due to my parents, who (despite still not knowing quite what I do) offer their unwavering support at every turn. To Mat, for his guidance and encouragement in writing this book, for his friendship, and for taking a chance on an eager stranger in 2019 – thank you for changing where I thought I was headed. And to Robin, who never stops inspiring, thank you for everything.

From Mat, thanks to Joe Bilsborough, Jonty Leibowitz, Sahil Dutta, and Nick Taylor for their comments on early chapter drafts and generous fertilising of many of the book's ideas and themes. One book during a pandemic is a stretch, two begins to look like unnecessary self-flagellation, but for their support, patience, and love throughout, thank you to my family and especially Carys; Somerset was wonderful, rain and all! Finally, to Adrienne. Given we communicated almost exclusively in ironic meme content for this book, it is a particular pleasure to say without irony: you're a real star, it has been a privilege to share this with you, and I am hugely excited to witness the wonderful things I know you will go on to do. Thank you.

From my side at least, this book is dedicated to the memory of Marshall Veniar (1984–2021), a true mensch, who passed away during the spring of 2021, but whose life taught those who knew and loved him how to live.

Notes

Introduction

1. Progressive International, 'Cuba Pledges "Lifesaving Package" of Covid-19 Vaccine Support to Global South at Progressive International Briefing', 25 January 2022.

2. Thomas Weidmann et al. (2020) 'Scientists' Warning on Affluence', *Nature Communications*, 11: 3107.

3. Harsha Walia (2021) *Border and Rule: Global Migration, Capitalism, and the Rise of Racist Nationalism*, Haymarket Books.

4. R. E. A. Almond, M. Grooten, and T. Petersen (eds) (2020) *Living Planet Report 2020 – Bending the Curve of Biodiversity Loss*, WWF and the Zoological Society of London.

5. Yinon M. Bar-On, Rob Phillips, and Ron Milo (2018) 'The Biomass Distribution on Earth', *Proceedings of the National Academy of Sciences of the United States of America*, Vol. 115 (25): 6506–11.

6. Matthew Green, 'Scientists Amazed as Canadian Permafrost Thaws Seventy Years Early', *Reuters*, 18 June 2019.

7. Sarah Boseley, 'Rising Antibiotic Resistance Increasing Risks of Routine Surgery – Study', *The Guardian*, 16 October 2015.

8. Cédric Durand, '1979 in Reverse', *Sidecar*, 1 June 2021.

9. Aaron Benanav (2020) *Automation and the Future of Work*, Verso Books.

10. William Callison and Zachary Manfredi (eds) (2019) *Mutant Neoliberalism: Market Rule and Political Rupture*, Fordham University Press.

11. Amna A. Akbar, 'Demands for a Democratic Political Economy', *Harvard Law Review Forum*, 1 December 2020.

12. R. S. Foa et al. (2020) *Youth and Satisfaction with Democracy*, University of Cambridge Bennett Institute for Public Policy.

13. This is the principle of 'politically active theory', as defined by Lea Ypi (2011) *Global Justice and Avant-Garde Political Agency*, Oxford University Press.

1: Ownership Matters

1. By 'Anglo-American capitalism', we mean those economies which emerged from imperial origins and benefit from our hierarchical global economy. They are defined by concentrated private ownership; corporation-dominated enterprise; outsize financial power; a coercive fusion of state and capital interests; and liberalised, unequal labour markets. While the term specifically refers to the economic arrangements of the US and UK, it includes, to varying degrees, many of the world's high-income economies.

2. Rashmi Dyal-Chand, 'Property, Collectivity, and Restraint', *Law and Political Economy Project*, 28 January 2021.

3. Laurie Macfarlane, 'To Solve the Housing Crisis, We Need to Fix Our Broken Land Economy', *openDemocracy*, 23 August 2017.

4. Andrew Cumbers and Thomas M. Hanna, 'Democratic Ownership: A Primer', *openDemocracy*, 11 March 2019.

5. Bruce G. Carruthers and Laura Ariovich (2004) 'The Sociology of Property Rights', *Annual Review of Sociology*, Vol. 30: 23–46.

6. Timothy Mitchell (2001) *Rule of Experts: Egypt, Techno-Politics, Modernity*, University of California Press.

7. Fabienne Orsi (2014) 'Rehabilitating Property as a Bundle of Rights: From its Origins to Elinor Ostrom, and Beyond?' *Revue internationale de droit économique*, Vol. 3: 387–99.

8. A. M. Honoré, 'Ownership', in Anthony Guest (ed) (1961) *Oxford Essays in Jurisprudence: A Collaborative Work*, Oxford University Press.

9. Martin O'Neill (2021) 'Justice, Power, and Participatory Socialism: On Piketty's Capital and Ideology', *Analyse & Kritik*, Vol. 43 (1): 89–124.

10. Liam B. Murphy and Thomas Nagel (2004) *The Myth of Ownership: Taxes and Justice*, Oxford University Press.

11. J. W. Mason, 'It's Bargaining Power All the Way Down', *Crooked Timber*, 15 December 2015.

12. Ibid.

13. Andrew Gamble and Gavin Kelly (1996) 'The New Politics of Ownership', *New Left Review*, Vol. 220 (1): 75.

14. Katharina Pistor, 'Liberal Property Law vs. Capitalism', *LPE Project Blog*, 27 January 2021.

15. Mike Davis interview with Sharif Abdel Kouddous, 'Mike Davis on Pandemics, Super-Capitalism and the Struggles of Tomorrow', *Madamasr*, 30 March 2020.

16. G. A. Cohen (1981) 'Freedom, Justice and Capitalism', *New Left Review*, Vol. 126 (1): 10.

17. William Clare Roberts (2016) *Marx's Inferno: The Political Theory of Capital*, Princeton University Press.

18. Corey Robin (2017) *The Reactionary Mind: Conservatism from Edmund Burke to Donald Trump*, Oxford University Press.

19. Kathi Weeks (2011) *The Problem with Work: Feminism, Marxism, Antiwork Politics and Postwork Imaginaries*, Duke University Press.

20. Erik Olin Wright (2019) *How to Be an Anticapitalist in the Twenty-First Century*, Verso Books.

21. Hadas Thier (2020) *A People's Guide to Capitalism: An Introduction to Marxist Economics*, Haymarket Books.

22. Nancy Fraser (2014) 'Behind Marx's Hidden Abode: For an Expanded Conception of Capitalism', *New Left Review*, Vol. 86 (2): 58.

23. Erik Olin Wright (2010) *Envisioning Real Utopias*, Verso Books.

24. Sarah Arnold, Aidan Harper, and Alfie Stirling (2021) 'The UK's Living Standards Crisis: The Case for a Living Income', *New Economics Foundation*.

25. Child Poverty Action Group (2021) 'Child Poverty Facts and Figures', https://cpag.org.uk/child-poverty/child-poverty-facts-and-figures

26. For a detailed discussion of the commonplace misrepresentation and exaggeration of 'progress' in areas such as global poverty, see: Rodrigo Aguilera (2020) *The Glass Half-Empty: Debunking the Myth of Progress in the Twenty -First Century*, Repeater Books.

27. Federal Reserve (2021) 'Distribution of Household Wealth in the U.S. since 1989', dataset, last updated 17 December 2021.

28. Trades Union Congress, Common Wealth, and High Pay Centre (2022) 'Do Dividends Pay Our Pensions?'.

29. Federal Reserve, 'Distribution of Household Wealth'.

30. Trades Union Congress, 'Do Dividends Pay Our Pensions?'.

31. Karl Marx (1867) *Capital: Volume 1*, Chapter 6.

32. Fraser, 'Behind Marx's Hidden Abode'.

33. Ibid.

34. Jason W. Moore and Raj Patel (2017) *A History of the World in Seven Cheap Things: A Guide to Capitalism, Nature, and the Future of the Planet*, Verso Books.

35. Fraser, 'Behind Marx's Hidden Abode'.

36. Thea Riofrancos (2020) *Resource Radicals: From Petro-Nationalism to Post -Extractivism in Ecuador*, Duke University Press.

37. Walter Rodney (1972) *How Europe Underdeveloped Africa*, Bogle-L'Ouverture Publications.

38. Karl Marx (1867) *Capital: Volume 3*.

39. Fraser, 'Behind Marx's Hidden Abode'.

40. See Sandy Hager (2015) 'Corporate Ownership of the Public Debt: Mapping the New Aristocracy of Finance', *Socio-Economic Review*, Vol. 13 (3): 505–23.

41. Fraser, 'Behind Marx's Hidden Abode'.

42. Gargi Bhattacharyya (2018) *Rethinking Racial Capitalism: Questions of Reproduction and Survival*, Rowman & Littlefield; Nancy Fraser, 'Is Capitalism Necessarily Racist?', *Politics/Letters*, 20 May 2019.

43. Gillian B. White, 'The Recession Had a Racial Slant', *The Atlantic*, 24 June 2015.

44. Ailsa Chan, Christopher Intagliata, and Jonaki Mehta, 'Black Homebuyers Today Pay an Unequal Price', *NPR*, 7 May 2021.

45. Bhattacharyya, *Rethinking Racial Capitalism*.

46. Katia Valenzuela-Fuentes, Esteban Alarcón-Barrueto, and Robinson Torres Salinas (2021) 'From Resistance to Creation: Socio-Environmental Activism in Chile's "Sacrifice Zones"', *Sustainability*, Vol. 13 (6): 34–81.

47. Robin Kelley and Charisse Burden-Stelly, 'Black and Red: Socialism and Black Liberation with Robin Kelley and Charisse Burden-Stelly', *Verso Blog*, 30 March 2021.

2: The Primacy of Property

1. Quoted in Steven Rattner 'Volcker Asserts US Must Trim Living Standard', *The New York Times*, 18 October 1979.

2. Quinn Slobodian (2018) *Globalists: The End of Empire and the Birth of Neoliberalism*, Harvard University Press.

3. Giovanni Arrighi (2003) 'The Social and Political Economy of Global-Turbulence', *New Left Review*, Vol. 20 (2): 5–71; Adom Getachew (2019) *Worldmaking After Empire: The Rise and Fall of Self-Determination*, Princeton University Press.

4. Slobodian, *Globalists*.

5. William Davies (2014) *The Limits of Neoliberalism: Authority, Sovereignty and the Logic of Competition*, SAGE Publications.

6. J. W. Mason, 'The Market Police', *Boston Review*, 1 June 2018.

7. Durand, '1979 in Reverse'.

8. Named after former chair of the Federal Reserve, Paul Volcker.

9. Tim Barker (2019) 'Other People's Blood', *n+1*, Issue 34.

10. Lucas Chanel et al. (2022) *World Inequality Report 2022*, World Inequality Database.

11. Yakov Feygin, 'The Deflationary Bloc', *Phenomenal World*, 9 January 2021.

12. Lisa Adkins, Melinda Cooper, and Martijn Konings (2020) *The Asset Economy*, Wiley.

13. Cassie Barton (2020) 'GE2019: How Did Demographics Affect the Result?', House of Commons Library.

14. Robert Brenner (2006) *The Economics of Global Turbulence: The Advanced Capitalist Economies from Long Boom to Long Downturn, 1945–2005*, Verso Books.

15. Sam Gindin and Leo Panitch (2013) *The Making of Global Capitalism: The Political Economy of American Empire*, Verso Books.

16. Martijn Konings, 'The Time of Finance', *LA Review of Books*, 28 December 2017.

17. Ibid.

18. Brett Christophers (2020) *Rentier Capitalism: Who Owns the Economy, and Who Pays for It?*, Verso Books.

19. Javier Moreno Zacarés (2021) 'Euphoria of the Rentier?', *New Left Review*, Vol. 129 (2): 47–67.

20. Brett Christophers, 'Class, Assets and Work in Rentier Capitalism', *Historical Materialism*, 19 March 2021.

21. Benanav, *Automation and the Future of Work*.

22. See, for example, Barton, 'GE2019, Adkins et al., *The Asset Economy*.

23. Trades Union Congress, Common Wealth, and High Pay Centre (2022) 'Do Dividends Pay Our Pensions?'.

24. Ned Davis Research, *Charts of the Decade: Fifteen Charts That Tell the Story of the 2010s*, 6 January 2020.

25. Mathew Lawrence et al. (2020) *Commoning the Company*, Common Wealth.

26. Edward Yardeni and Mali Quintana, 'Central Banks: Monthly Balance Sheets', Yardeni Research, Inc., 10 August 2021.

27. Andrew Bailey et al., 'The Central Bank Balance Sheet As a Policy Tool: Past, Present and Future', Bank of England, Paper prepared for the Jackson Hole Economic Policy Symposium, 27–28 August 2020.

28. Joel Rabinovich, 'Have Non-Financial Businesses Generally Turned to Financial Investments for Profits?', *Notes on the Crises*, 24 March 2020.

29. Iñaki Aldasoro, Bryan Hardy, and Nikola Tarashev (2021) 'Corporate Debt: Post-GFC through the Pandemic', *BIS Quarterly Review*, 7 June 2021.

30. Ned Davis Research, 2020.

31. J. P. Morgan Asset Management, 'Guide to the Markets: US 2Q 2020, As of June 1, 2020'.

32. Carlos Cantú et al. (2021) *A Global Database on Central Banks' Monetary Responses to Covid-19*, BIS Working Papers No. 934.

33. Jeffrey Cheng et al. 'What's the Fed Doing in Response to the Covid-19 Crisis? What More Could it Do?', Brookings Institute, 30 March 2021.

34. Alex Woodward, 'The World's Billionaires Added $5 Trillion to Their Wealth during the Pandemic, the Biggest Surge in Decades', *The Independent*, 7 April 2021.

35. Frank van Lervenk, 'Public Debt – The Untold Story', New Economics Foundation blog, 26 May 2021.

36. Eben Shapiro, 'Former Treasury Secretary Larry Summers on Inflation Worries, Cryptocurrency and "Our Greatest Long-Term Threat"', *TIME*, 6 June 2021.

3: Engines of Extraction

1. Quoted in Francesco Guerrera, 'Welch Condemns Share Price Focus', *The Financial Times*, 12 March 2009.

2. Peter Whoriskey, Douglas MacMillan, and Jonathan O'Connell, '"Doomed to Fail": Why a $4 Trillion Bailout Couldn't Revive the American Economy', *Washington Post*, 5 October 2020.

3. Christine Williamson, 'BlackRock CEO Larry Fink Sees 18 Percent Pay Rise', *Pensions and Investment Online*, 2 April 2021.

4. Josh Barro, @jbarro, 'I know people think this is fun', Twitter, January 27, 2021, https://twitter.com/jbarro/status/1354464982981877762

5. Doug Henwood (1997) *Wall Street: How it Works and For Whom*, Verso Books.

6. Ibid.

7. J. W. Mason, 'Disgorge the Cash', *The New Inquiry*, 21 April 2014.

8. Ibid.

9. Alexis Goldstein, 'What happened with GameStop?', *Markets Weekly*, 28 January 2021.

10. World Bank, 'COVID-19 to Add as Many as 150 Million Extreme Poor by 2021', press release, 7 October 2020.

11. James Manyika et al. (2021) 'A New Look at How Corporations Impact the Economy and Households', McKinsey Global Institute discussion paper.

12. Shin et al. (2018) 'Tracking the International Footprints of Global Firms', *BIS Quarterly Review*, March 2018.

13. Henwood, *Wall Street*.

14. Sanjukta Paul, 'The Allocation of Economic Coordination Rights', *Law and Political Economy Project*, 21 September 2018.

15. Adam Winkler, '"Corporations Are People" Is Built on an Incredible 19th -Century Lie', *The Atlantic*, 5 March 2018.

16. Isabelle Ferreras (2017) *Firms as Political Entities: Saving Democracy through Economic Bicameralism*, Cambridge University Press.

17. Karl Marx (1867) *Capital: Volume 3*.

18. J. W. Mason, 'Karl Marx and the Corporation', *Jacobin*, 5 July 2020.

19. Nicole Aschoff (2019) 'Do Managers Rule?', *Catalyst*, Vol. 2 (4).

20. Mason, 'Karl Marx and the Corporation'.

21. Paddy Ireland (2018) 'Efficiency or Power? The Rise of the Shareholder-Oriented Joint Stock Corporation', *Indiana Journal of Global Legal Studies*, Vol. 25 (1): 291–330.

22. Adolf Berle and Gardiner Means (1932) *The Modern Corporation and Private Property*, Transaction Publishers.

23. Ireland, 'Efficiency or Power?'.

24. Henwood, *Wall Street*.

25. Ann Pettifor (2017) *The Production of Money: How to Break the Power of Bankers*, Verso Books.

26. See, for example, John Kenneth Gailbraith (1967) *The New Industrial State*, Princeton University Press; Paul Sweezy and Paul A. Baran (1966) *Monopoly Capital: An Essay on the American Economic and Social Order*, Monthly Review Press.

27. Mason, 'Disgorge the Cash'.

28. Samuel Knafo and Sahil Jai Dutta (2019) 'The Myth of the Shareholder Revolution and the Financialization of the Firm', *Review of International Political Economy*, Vol. 27 (3): 476–99.

29. Benjamin Braun (2020) 'Asset Manager Capitalism as a Corporate Governance Regime', SocArVix.

30. Mason, 'Disgorge the Cash'; Lawrence et al., 'Commoning the Company'.

31. Mariana Mazzucato (2018) *The Value of Everything: Making and Taking in the Global Economy*, Allen Lane.

32. William Lazonick, 'Profits Without Prosperity', *Harvard Business Review*, September 2014.

33. Ireland, 'Efficiency or Power?'.

34. Joel Rabinovich, 'Have Non-Financial Businesses Generally Turned to Financial Investments for Profits?', *Notes on the Crises*, 24 March 2020.

35. Ibid.

36. Knafo and Dutta, 'The Myth of the Shareholder Revolution'.

37. Rafael La Porta et al. (2000) 'Investor Protection and Corporate Governance', *Journal of Financial Economics*, Vol. 58 (1).

38. Braun, 'Asset Manager Capitalism'.

39. Crystal Kim, 'The ETF Business Is Dominated by the Big Three. The SEC Is Suddenly Concerned', *Barron's*, 5 April 2019.

40. Braun, 'American Asset Manager Capitalism'.

41. Mazzucato *The Value of Everythin*, p. 159.

42. The Economist: Leaders, 'Masters of the Universe: The Rise of the Financial Machines', *The Economist*, 5 October 2019.

43. Chris Hayes (2021) *Passive Attack: Charting the Rise of Passive Index Trackers*, Common Wealth.

44. Annie Massa and Caleb Melby, 'In Fink We Trust: BlackRock Is Now the Fourth Branch of Government', *Bloomberg*, 5 May 2020.

45. Ibid.

46. Angharad Carrick, 'Private Equity Gets Creative as It Sits on Record Dry Powder Pile', *City AM*, 2 December 2020.

47. Eileen Appelbaum and Rosemary Batt (2014) *Private Equity at Work: When Wall Street Manages Main Street*, Russell Sage Foundation.

48. Sanjukta Paul, 'On Socialising the Constitution of Economic Coordination', *Law and Political Economy Project*, 29 June 2020.

49. Katharina Pistor (2019) *The Code of Capital: How the Law Creates Wealth and Inequality*, Princeton University Press.

50. Simon Deakin, 'The Evolution of Corporate Form: From Shareholders' Property to the Corporation as Commons', in Thomas Clarke, Justin O'Brien, and Charles R. T. O'Kelley (eds) (2019) *The Oxford Handbook of the Corporation*, Oxford University Press.

51. For further development of these five principles, see Marjorie Kelly (2012) *Owning Our Future: The Emerging Ownership Revolution*, Berrett-Koehler Publishers.

52. Robert Hockett (2019) 'Finance without Financiers', *Politics & Society*, Vol. 47 (4): 491–527.

53. Isabella Weber, 'Could Strategic Price Controls Help Fight Inflation?' *The Guardian*, 29 December 2021.

54. Katharina Pistor (2020) 'Theorizing Beyond "The Code of Capital": A Reply', *Accounting, Economics, and Law: A Convivium*, Vol. 11 (1).

55. Paul, 'On Socialising the Constitution of Economic Coordination'.

56. Pistor, *Code of Capital*, Chapter 6.

57. Jedediah Britton-Purdy et al. (2020) 'Building a Law-and-Political-Economy Framework: Beyond the Twentieth-Century Synthesis', *The Yale Law Journal*, Vol. 129 (6): 1784–832.

58. Ellen Meiksins Wood (1999) *The Origin of Capitalism*, Verso Books.

59. Leigh Phillips and Michal Rozworski (2019) *The People's Republic of Walmart: How the World's Biggest Corporations Are Laying the Foundation for Socialism*, Verso Books.

60. Robin Murray (1987) 'Ownership, Control and the Market', *New Left Review*, Vol. 164 (Jul/Aug): 87–112.

61. Diane Elson (1988) 'Market Socialism or Socialization of the Market?', *New Left Review*, Vol. 172 (Nov/Dec): 3–44.

62. See Dutta et al. (forthcoming 2022) *Unprecedented? How Covid-19 Exposed the Politics of the Economy*, MIT Press.

63. Hockett, 'Finance without Financiers'.

64. Pettifor, *The Production of Money*.

4: Cracks in the Foundation

1. David Sirota and Andrew Perez, 'Blackstone CEO Celebrates "Huge Increases in Rents" as Millions Face Eviction', *Jacobin*, 14 December 2020.

2. Joe Bilsborough, 'Rentier Island', *Tribune*, 14 March 2021.

3. Rob Merrick, 'Covid Stamp Duty Holiday Cost £6.4bn and Helped Rich House Buyers in South, Analysts Say', *The Independent*, 23 November 2021.

4. Ibid.

5. Lisa Adkins, Melinda Cooper, and Martijn Konings (2020) *The Asset Economy*, Wiley.

6. Alana Semuels, 'When Wall Street Is Your Landlord', *The Atlantic*, 13 February 2019.

7. Ryan Dezember, 'If You Sell a House These Days the Buyer Might Be a Pension Fund', *The Wall Street Journal*, 4 April 2021.

8. Brett Christophers (2021) 'How and Why US Single-Family Housing Became an Investor Asset Class', *Journal of Urban History*, July.

9. Sirota and Perez, 'Blackstone CEO Celebrates "Huge Increases in Rents"'.

10. Diane Burns et al. (2016) *Where Does the Money Go? Financialised Chains and the Crisis in Residential Care*, Manchester University Centre for Research on Socio-Cultural Change.

11. Melinda Cooper (2017) Family Values, Zone Books; Adkins et al., *The Asset Economy*.

12. Martin Arnold, Colby Smith, and Matthew Rocco, 'House Prices Climb to Record Levels in US and Europe', *The Financial Times*, 22 June 2021.

13. Josh Ryan-Collins, 'Is the UK Housing Bubble about to Burst? These Are the Best and Worst Scenarios', *The Guardian*, 2 July 2021.

14. Office of National Statistics (2018) *Statistical Bulletin: Wealth in Great Britain Wave 5: 2014 to 2016*.

15. See, for example, Keeanga-Yamahtta Taylor (2019) *Race for Profit: How Banks and the Real Estate Industry Undermined Black Homeownership*, University of North Carolina Press.

16. Ryan-Collins, 'Is the UK Housing Bubble about to Burst?'.

17. Robert Booth, 'About 700,000 Renters Served with 'No-Fault' Eviction Notices since Start of Pandemic', *The Guardian*, 15 April 2021.

18. Rupert Jones, 'Private Rents in Britain Rise at Fastest Rate on Record', *The Guardian*, 27 January 2022.

19. Adkins et al., *The Asset Economy*.

20. Ibid.

21. Ibid.

22. https://www.hse.gov.uk/migrantworkers/healthcare.htm

23. Isaac Stanley, Adrienne Buller, and Mathew Lawrence (2021) *Caring for the Earth, Caring for Each Other: An Industrial Strategy for Adult Social Care*, Common Wealth.

24. For further detail, see Burns et al., *Where Does the Money Go?*.

25. Christine Corlet Walker, 'Care Homes: Why Investment Firms Can Be Bad Owners', *The Conversation*, 12 April 2021.

26. Fiona Williams, 'Towards a Transnational Analysis of the Political Economy of Care', in R. Mahon and F. Williamson (eds) (2012) *Feminist Ethics and Social Policy: Towards a New Global Political Economy of Care*, University of British Columbia Press, pp. 21–38.

27. Julie Froud et al. (2020) '(How) Does Productivity Matter in the Foundational Economy?', *Local Economy*, Vol. 35 (4): 316–36.

28. Stanley et al., 'Caring for the Earth'.

29. Ibid.

30. The Care Collective (2020) *Care Manifesto: The Politics of Interdependence*, Verso Books.

31. Emma Dowling (2021) *The Care Crisis: What Caused It and How Can We End It?*, Verso Books.

32. Amia Srinivasan (2021) *The Right to Sex*, Bloomsbury.

33. Burns et al., *Where Does the Money Go?*.

34. Susan Ferguson (2020) *Women and Work Feminism, Labour, and Social Reproduction*, Pluto Books; Tithi Bhattacharya (2017) *Social Reproduction Theory: Remapping Class, Recentering Oppression*, Pluto Books.

35. Emma Dowling, 'Money Alone Won't Fix the Care Crisis – We Need a Radical Rethink', *Novara Media*, 29 September 2020.

36. Gabriel Winant (2021) *The Next Shift: The Fall of Industry and the Rise of Health Care in Rust Belt America*, Harvard University Press.

37. Thomas M. Hanna et al. (2021) *Democratic Digital Infrastructure*, Common Wealth.

38. Miranda Hall et al. (2019) *Full Fibre Futures*, Common Wealth.

39. Ibid.

40. Ben Tarnoff (2022) *Internet for the People: A Manifesto*, Verso Books.

41. Hall et al. (2019) *Full Fibre Futures*.

42. Frontier Economics (2018) *Future Telecoms Infrastructure Review*, Annex A.

43. Thomas M. Hanna and Joe Guinan, 'Privatisation, a Very British Disease', *openDemocracy*, 5 November 2013.

44. Massimo Florio (2004) *The Great Divestiture: Evaluating the Welfare Impact of the British Privatizations, 1979–1997*, MIT Press.

45. Thomas M. Hanna (2018) *Our Common Wealth: The Return of Public Ownership in the United States*, Manchester University Press.

46. Ibid.

47. J. W. Mason, 'Climate Policy from a Keynesian Perspective', *New European*, 21 December 2021.

5: A Shared Inheritance

1. Thomas M. Hanna, Miriam Brett, and Dana Brown (2020) *Democratising Knowledge: Transforming Intellectual Property and R&D*, Common Wealth.

2. For a robust, evidenced discussion of this phenomenon, see Mariana Mazzucato (2013) *The Entrepreneurial State*, Anthem Press.

3. Sydney Lupkin, 'A Decade Marked by Outrage Over Drug Prices', *NPR*, 31 December 2019.

4. Inmaculada Hernandez et al. (2020) 'Changes in List Prices, Net Prices, and Discounts for Branded Drugs in the US, 2007–2018', *JAMA*, Vol. 323 (9): 854–62.

5. Darby Herkert et al. (2019) 'Cost-Related Insulin Underuse among Patients with Diabetes', *JAMA Internal Medicine*, Vol. 179 (1): 112–14.

6. Rosie Collington, 'Who Benefits When the Price of Insulin Soars?', *INET*, 16 April 2020.

7. William Lazonick, 'Profits without Prosperity', *Harvard Business Review*, September 2014.

8. Margarida Jorge, 'The Opioid Crisis Reflects Larger Big Pharma Norms', *Morning Consult*, 3 October 2019.

9. Collington, 'Who Benefits When the Price of Insulin Soars?'

10. Sharif Abdel Kouddous interviews Mike Davis, 'Mike Davis on Pandemics, Super-Capitalism and the Struggles of Tomorrow', *Madamasr*, 30 March 2020.

11. Jodi Kantor, Karen Weise, and Grace Ashford, 'The Amazon That Customers Don't See', *The New York Times*, 15 June 2021.

12. Colin Lecher, 'How Amazon Automatically Tracks and Fires Warehouse Workers for "Productivity"', *The Verge*, 25 April 2019.

13. Will Evans, 'How Amazon Hid Its Safety Crisis', *Reveal*, 29 September 2020.

14. Kantor et al., 'The Amazon That Customers Don't See'.

15. Brett Christophers (2020) *Rentier Capitalism: Who Owns the Economy, and Who Pays for It?*, Verso Books.

16. This is when the value derived from using a platform depends on the number of others using it, which incentivises concentration and consolidation.

17. Christophers (2020) *Rentier Capitalism*.

18. Nathan Tankus, 'The Stock Market Is Less Disconnected from the "Real Economy" than You Think', *Notes on the Crises*, 24 September 2020.

19. Ibid.

20. William Davies (2021) 'The Politics of Recognition in the Age of Social Media', *New Left Review*, Vol. 128 (Mar/Apr): 90.

21. Shoshana Zuboff (2018) *The Age of Surveillance Capitalism: The Fight for a Human Future at the New Frontier of Power*, Harvard University Press.

22. Ameen Kamlana, 'Your Medical Records Are About to Be Given Away. As GPs, We're Fighting Back', *The Guardian*, 3 June 2021.

23. Zuboff, *The Age of Surveillance Capitalism*.

24. Salomé Viljoen, 'Data as Property?', *Phenomenal World*, 16 October 2020.

25. Ibid.

26. McKinsey & Company, 'How COVID-19 Has Pushed Companies over the Technology Tipping Point – and Transformed Business Forever', 5 October 2020'; James Meadway, 'Coronavirus Will Require Us to Completely Reshape the Economy', *Novara Media*, 16 March 2020.

27. Aaron Benanav (2020) *Automation and the Future of Work*, Verso Books.

28. Mike Davis (2005) *Planet of Slums*, Verso Books.

29. Benanav, *Automation and the Future of Work*.

30. Adam Greenfield (2017) *Radical Technologies: The Design of Everyday Life*, Verso Books.

31. Endnotes, 'Error', Issue 5.

32. Harry Braverman (1974) *Labor and Monopoly Capital*, Monthly Review Press.

33. Sarah T. Hamid (2020) 'Community Defense: Sarah T. Hamid on Abolishing Carceral Technologies', *Logic*, Issue 11.

34. Tuberculosis, despite the availability of effective drugs, remains one of the world's deadliest diseases. Primarily affecting lower-income countries, development of affordable alternatives or waiving patents to improve access have been stymied. See: https://www.doctorswithoutborders.org/what-we-do/news -stories/news/tuberculosis-drug-remains-too-expensive-despite-new-price

35. Brett Christophers (2021) 'Fossilised Capital: Price and Profit in the Energy Transition', *New Political Economy*, Vol. 27 (1).

36. Martín Arboleda (2020) *Planetary Mine: Territories of Extraction under Late Capitalism*, Verso Books.

37. Viljoen, 'Data as Property?'.

38. Developing a network of 'data trusts', institutions for democratically organising data by and for the benefit of defined communities, whether by place, social mission, or industry, with data analysis driven by needs not accumulation, can start this process.

39. Jonathan Gray (2018) 'Three Aspects of Data Worlds', *Krisis*, Issue 1.

40. Salomé Viljoen, 'Democratic Data: A Relational Theory for Data Governance', *Yale Law Journal*, 23 November 2020.

41. Thomas M. Hanna, Nils Peters, and Mathew Lawrence (2020) *A Common Platform*, Common Wealth.

42. Hanna, Brown, Brett, *Democratising Knowledge*.

43. Benanav, *Automation and the Future of Work*.

44. John Merrick, '"Nobody Knows More about Running This Country Than Me": James Boggs and the Racial Politics of Automation', *Autonomy*, 10 May 2021.

45. Martin Hägglund (2019) *This Life: Secular Faith and Spiritual Freedom*, Pantheon Books.

46. Benanav, *Automation and the Future of Work*.

6: Robbing the Worker and the Soil

1. Rebecca Ratcliffe, '"This Place Used to Be Green": The Brutal Impact of Oil in the Niger Delta', *The Guardian*, 6 December 2019.

2. Anna Bruederle and Roland Hodler (2019) 'Effect of Oil Spills on Infant Mortality in Nigeria', *Proceedings of the National Academy of Sciences of the United States of America*, Vol. 116 (12).

3. Amnesty International (2017) *Nigeria: A Criminal Enterprise? Shell's Involvement in Human Rights Violations in Nigeria in the 1990s*.

4. Ibid.

5. Alberto Acosta (2013) 'Extractivism and Neoextractivism: Two Sides of the Same Curse', *The New International*. https://www.tni.org/files/download/beyonddevelopment_extractivism.pdf

6. Shell, 'Shell Accelerates Drive for Net-Zero Emissions with Customer-First Strategy', press release, 11 February 2021, https://www.shell.com/media/news-and-media-releases/2021/shell-accelerates-drive-for-net-zero-emissions-with-customer-first-strategy.html

7. ActionAid (2015) *Caught in the Net: How 'Net-Zero Emissions' Will Delay Real Climate Action and Drive Land Grabs*. See also: Kristen Lyons and Peter Westoby (2014) 'Carbon Colonialism and the New Land Grab: Plantation Forestry in Uganda and its Livelihood Impacts', *Journal of Rural Studies* Vol. 36: 13–21.

8. Laura Hurst, 'Shell Green Plans under Scrutiny as Investors Demand More Action', *Bloomberg*, 18 May 2021.

9. Thea Riofrancos (2021) 'The Rush to "Go Electric" Comes with a Hidden Cost: Destructive Lithium Mining', *The Guardian*, 14 June 2021.

10. Andreas Malm and the Zetkin Collective (2021) *White Skin, Black Fuel: On the Danger of Fossil Fascism*. Verso Books.

11. Ibid.

12. Valerie Landrieu, 'Jordan Bardella: Le meilleur allie de l'ecologies, c'est la frontiere', *Les Echos*, 7 April 2019. Via Malm and the Zetkin Collective, *White Skin, Black Fuel*.

13. Ulrich Brand and Markus Wissen (2017) *The Imperial Mode of Living*, Verso Books, pp. 39–40.

14. Ken Henshaw et al. (2017) *Beyond Oil: Reimagining Development in the Niger Delta*, Health of Mother Earth Foundation.

15. Ibid.

16. Martín Arboleda (2020) *Planetary Mine: Territories of Extraction under Late Capitalism*, Verso Books.

17. Eniko Horvath and Amanda Romero Medina, 'Indigenous People's Livelihoods at Risk in Scramble for Lithium, the New White Gold', *Reuters*, 9 April 2019.

18. Damian Carrington, 'Is Deep Sea Mining Vital for a Greener Future – Even if It Destroys Ecosystems?', *The Guardian*, 4 June 2017.

19. Martín Arboleda, *Planetary Mine*.

20. Anna Gross, 'Carbon Offset Market Progresses during Coronavirus', *The Financial Times*, 29 September 2020.

21. Kevin Anderson (2012), 'The Inconvenient Truth of Carbon Offsets', *Nature*, 4 April 2012.

22. Doreen Stabinsky (2020) *Nature-Based Solutions or Nature-Based Seductions?*, Third World Network and The African Centre for Biodiversity.

23. Ben Elgin, 'These Trees Are Not What They Seem: How the Nature Conservancy, the World's Biggest Environmental Group, Became a Dealer of Meaningless Carbon Offsets', *Bloomberg Green*, 9 December 2020.

24. Stephen Stapczynski, Akshat Rathi, and Godfrey Marawanyika, 'How to Sell "Carbon Neutral" Fossil Fuel That Doesn't Exist', *Bloomberg*, 11 August 2021.

25. ActionAid (2021) *Shell's Net Zero Plans Need Land up to Three Times the Size of the Netherlands for Carbon Offsets*.

26. Frederic Simon, 'IEA Criticised over Growing Share of Bioenergy in Net Zero Scenario', *Euractiv*, 18 May 2021.

27. ActionAid (2021) *Shell's Net Zero Plans*.

28. Lyons and Westoby, 'Carbon Colonialism'.

29. Daniela Gabor (2020) 'The Wall Street Climate Consensus', *Tax Justice Network: Focus*, Vol. 11 (3).

30. Green Finance Observatory (2021) *Eight Questions about the Global Standard for Nature-Based Solutions*.

31. Katie Kedward, Josh Ryan-Collins, and Hugues Chenet (2020) *Managing Nature-Related Financial Risks: A Precautionary Policy Approach for Central Banks and Financial Supervisors*, UCL Institute for Innovation and Public Purpose Working Paper.

32. International Energy Agency (2020), *World Energy Investment 2020*.

33. Jillian Ambrose (2021) 'North Sea Oil Was Battered by Covid, but Now Faces Much Deadlier Waves', *The Guardian*, 29 August 2021.

34. Brett Christophers (2021) 'Fossilised Capital: Price and Profit in the Energy Transition', *New Political Economy*, Vol. 27 (1).

35. Katie Gallogly-Swan and Miriam Brett (2020) *A Climate Retrofit for UK Trade*, Common Wealth.

36. Thea Riofrancos (2021) 'The Rush to "Go Electric" Comes with a Hidden Cost: Destructive Lithium Mining', *The Guardian*, 14 June 2021.

37. Joel Millward-Hopkins et al. (2020) 'Providing Decent Living with Minimum Energy: A Global Scenario', *Global Environmental Change*, Vol. 65.

38. Jefim Vogel et al. (2021) 'Socio-Economic Conditions for Satisfying Human Needs at Low Energy Use: An International Analysis of Social Provisioning', *Global Environmental Change*, Vol. 69.

39. J. K. Steinberger et al. (2020) 'Scientists' Warning on Affluence', *Nature Climate Change*, https://www.nature.com/articles/s41467-020-16941-y

40. For a compelling empirical rebuke of the 'tragedy of the commons', see Elinor Ostrom's now seminal *Governing the Commons* (1990).

41. Kyle Frankel Davis et al. (2020) 'Tropical Forest Loss Enhanced by Large-Scale Land Acquisition', *Nature Geoscience*, Vol. 13: 482–88.

42. Gleb Raygorodetsky, 'Indigenous Peoples Defend Earth's Biodiversity – but They're in Danger,' *National Geographic*, 16 November 2018.

43. Brent Kaup and Paul Gellert (2017) 'Cycles of Resource Nationalism: Hegemonic Struggle and the Incorporation of Bolivia and Indonesia', *International Journal of Comparative Sociology*, Vol. 58 (4).

Conclusion

1. Astra Taylor (2019) *Democracy May Not Exist, but We'll Miss it When it's Gone*, Verso Books.

2. Erik Olin Wright (2006) 'Compass Points', *New Left Review*, Vol. 41 (Sep/Oct): 93–124.

3. See, for example, Thomas Dudley and Ethan Rouen, 'The Big Benefits of Employee Ownership', *Harvard Business Review*, 13 May 2021.

4. United Nations Conference on Trade and Development (2020) *Trade and Development Report*.

5. Sirio Aramonte (2020) 'Mind the Buybacks, Beware of the Leverage', *Bank for International Settlements Quarterly Review*.

6. Doug Henwood (1997) *Wall Street*, Verso Books.

7. See, for example, Adrienne Buller and Benjamin Braun (2021) *Under New Management: Share Ownership and the Growth of UK Asset Manager Capitalism*, Common Wealth; and J. W. Mason (2015) *Disgorge the Cash: The Disconnect between Corporate Borrowing and Investment*, Roosevelt Institute.

8. Isabel Ortiz et al. (eds) (2019) *Reversing Pension Privatizations: Rebuilding Public Pension Systems in Eastern Europe and Latin America*, International Labour Organization.

9. Mercer (2020) *Investing in the Future: European Asset Allocation Insights 2020*; Mercer (2019) *European Asset Allocation Survey*.

10. Replacement rate refers to the percentage of an individual's annual employment income that is replaced by retirement income when they retire.

11. Mark Blyth (2002) *Great Transformations*, Cambridge University Press.

12. Matthew Impelli, '"Bar Rescue" Host Jon Taffer Likens Unemployment Benefits to "Hungry, Obedient Dogs"', *Newsweek*, 13 August 2021.

13. Justin Bentham et al. (2013) *Manifesto for the Foundational Economy*, Manchester University Centre for Research on Socio-Cultural Change Working Paper No. 131.

14. Ibid.

15. For a wide-ranging discussion of alternative proposals, see Isaac Stanley, Adrienne Buller, and Mathew Lawrence (2021) *Caring for the Earth, Caring for Each Other: An Industrial Strategy for Adult Social Care*, Common Wealth.

16. Carlo Borzaga and Giulia Galera (2016) 'Innovating the Provision of Welfare Services through Collective Action: The Case of Italian Social Cooperatives', *International Review of Sociology*, Vol. 26 (1): 31–47.

17. Erika Solomon and George Hammond, 'My Flat Is Now a Commodity': Berlin to Vote on Seizing Rental Properties', *The Financial Times*, 10 August 2021.

18. Satoko Kishimoto, Olivier Petitjean, and Lavinia Steinfort (2018) *Reclaiming Public Services: How Cities and Citizens Are Turning Back Privatisation*, Transnational Institute.

19. Mathew Lawrence and Thomas H. Hanna (2020) *Ownership Futures: Towards Democratic Public Ownership in the 21st Century*, Common Wealth.

20. Robin McKie, 'Britons Reach Africans' Annual Carbon Emissions in Just Two Weeks', *The Guardian*, 5 January 2020; Karen McVeigh, 'West Accused of 'Climate Hypocrisy' as Emissions Dwarf Those of Poor Countries', *The Guardian*, 28 January 2022.

21. Joel Millward-Hopkins et al. (2020) 'Providing Decent Living with Minimum Energy: A Global Scenario', *Global Environmental Change*, Vol. 65 (Nov).

22. David Graeber (2012) 'Of Flying Cars and the Declining Rate of Profit', *The Baffler*, No. 19 (Mar).

23. Ibid.

24. Dorah Feliciano, 'CIMI: Brazilian Indigenous Land Invasions Rose 135 Percent in 2019', *The Rio Times*, 1 October 2020.

25. Kathryn Baragwanath and Ella Bayi (2020) 'Collective Property Rights Reduce Deforestation in the Brazilian Amazon', *Proceedings of the National Academy of Sciences of the United States of America*, Vol. 117 (34).

26. David Bray, Leticia Merino, and Deborah Barry (eds) (2005) *The Community Forests of Mexico: Managing for Sustainable Landscapes*, University of Texas Press.

27. Peter Burjorjee et al. (2017) 'Land Cooperatives as a Model for Sustainable Agriculture', *Blekinge Institute of Technology*.

28. Nature, 'Small Farms Outdo Big Ones on Biodiversity – and Crop Yields', *Nature Sustainability*, 29 March 2021; Max Ajl, 'How Much Will the US Way of Life © Have to Change?', *Uneven Earth*, June 2019.

29. Keir Milburn and Bertie Russell (2019) *Public-Common Partnerships: Building New Circuits of Collective Ownership*, Common Wealth.

30. Gleb Raygorodetsky, 'Indigenous Peoples Defend Earth's Biodiversity – but They're in Danger', *National Geographic*, 16 November 2018.

31. See, for example, Kyle Frankel Davis et al. (2020) 'Tropical Forest Loss Enhanced by Large-Scale Land Acquisitions', *Nature Geoscience* Vol. 13; Elinor Ostrom (1990) *Governing the Commons*, Cambridge University Press.

32. Johanna Bozuwa (2020) *The Case for Public Ownership of the Fossil Fuel Industry*, The Next System Project.

33. Ibid.

34. Andreas Malm (2016) *Fossil Capital: The Rise of Steam Power and the Roots of Global Warming*, Verso Books.

35. See, for example, Olúfẹ́mi O. Táíwò and Beba Cibralic, 'The Case for Climate Reparations', *Foreign Policy*, 10 October 2020; Keston K. Perry (2020) 'Realising Climate Reparations: Towards a Global Climate Stabilization Fund and Resilience Fund Programme for Loss and Damage in Marginalised and Former Colonised Societies', https://papers.ssrn.com/sol3/papers.cfm?abstract_id=3561121; Edward A. Page and Clare Heyward (2016) 'Compensating for Climate Change Loss and Damage', *Political Studies*, Vol. 65 (2): 356–72.

36. Thomas Piketty (2020) *Capital and Ideology*, Harvard University Press.

37. Rosa Luxemburg (1900) *Reform or Revolution*.

38. As Gramsci defined it in *Prison Notebooks*, a historic bloc is 'an alliance of different class forces politically organized around a set of hegemonic ideas that gave strategic direction and coherence to its constituent elements'.

39. Ulrich Brand and Markus Wissen (2017) *The Imperial Mode of Living*, Verso Books.

40. James C. Scott (1998) *Seeing Like a State*, Yale University Press.

41. Nicos Poulantzas (1978) 'Toward a Democratic Socialism', *New Left Review*, Vol. 109 (May/June): 80.

42. For more on the 'professional managerial class', and the coherence of a new historic bloc, see Gabriel Winant, 'Coronavirus and Chronopolitics', *n+1*, Issue 37, Spring 2020, and Gabriel Winant, 'Professional-Managerial Chasm', *n+1*, 10 October 2019.

43. Stuart Hall, 'Blue Election, Election Blues 1987', in Selected Political Writings, Sally Davison, David Featherstone, Michael Rustin, and Bill Schwarz (eds) (2017) *Selected Political Writings*, Duke University Press, pp. 238–47.

44. Rodrigo Nunes (2021) *Neither Vertical nor Horizontal A Theory of Political Organization*, Verso Books.

45. Alyssa Battistoni, 'On the Politics of Oil Abolition', *Abolition Democracy*, 5 March 2021.

46. Ibid.

47. Ibid.

48. As cited in Amia Srinivasan (2021) *The Right to Sex*, Bloomsbury.

Index